Introduction to DSLR
PHOTOGRAPHY
& Creating Better Photos

di Sogno

AF278839

Introduction to DSLR Photography
& Creating Better Photos

di Sogno
PHOTOGRAPHY

Tony Fiorda
Owner/Photographer
di Sogno Photography
1005 Alderman Drive
Alpharetta, GA 30005
770-817-0945

Introduction to DSLR Photography & Creating Better Photos

ISBN 978-0-9904160-0-5

Published by:

di Sogno Photography
1005 Alderman Drive
Alpharetta, GA 30005
770-817-0945

INTRODUCTION

Everyone wants their photos to capture what they did, where they went, and what they saw. Initially it looks easy; pick up the camera, point it at the scene and push the button. The image is captured for eternity. But later, as you look at the image, you start noticing that the scene looks a little washed out or the image is blurry when you wanted an image that is sharp as a tack. You may ask yourself, "How can I do it better?"

This book will help you learn how to take better photos as you learn to use the features of your DSLR camera. It will help you understand your camera better and provide new skills and techniques that will allow you to create better images that fully capture the emotion and action of the scene.

One of the most common questions I hear is "Which camera should I use to take better pictures?" I can tell you that it isn't necessarily the camera but the person behind it that will capture the better pictures. The camera is only a tool, and today just about any camera from a point and shoot to a professional digital single lens reflex camera (DSLR) will allow you to capture great images. It's all in how you use that tool and apply various techniques. In this book we'll discuss some of those techniques as well as a general workflow for use after capture of the images. We'll also discuss how to use your DSLR camera and a few accessories to help make your photography experiences better.

In the first and second parts you'll learn about the camera, review some of the technical stuff such as aperture and shutter speed settings, and rehash camera basics such as ISO, white balance, focus modes, depth of field, lenses and their effects, RAW or JPEG file types.

In the third part, we'll have some fun talking about the rules of composition and a few simple techniques for creating better photos. A pre-shoot checklist is presented along with the general rules of composition, and some shooting techniques for creating more interesting images.

The fourth part will present workflow options, what it is, how to create it and what a consistent workflow will do for you and your images. We'll discuss some of the applications that are available to augment that workflow.

At the completion of this book, you will have a better understanding of your camera, of the physical rules of photography, how to create better images using those rules, and how to utilize a repeatable workflow for your specific photographic needs. By gaining an understanding of these concepts you will improve your picture taking experience and see an overall improvement in your photography.

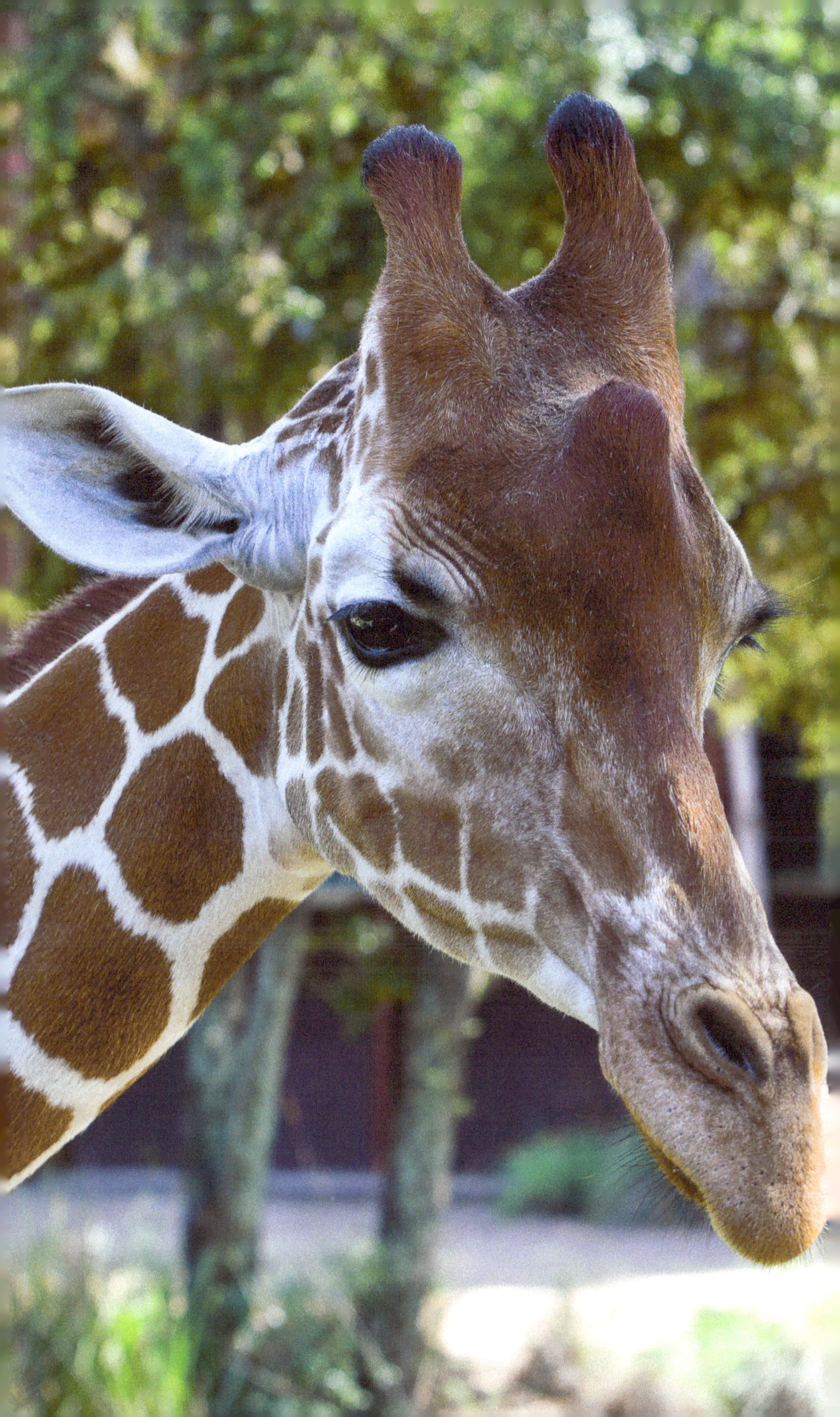

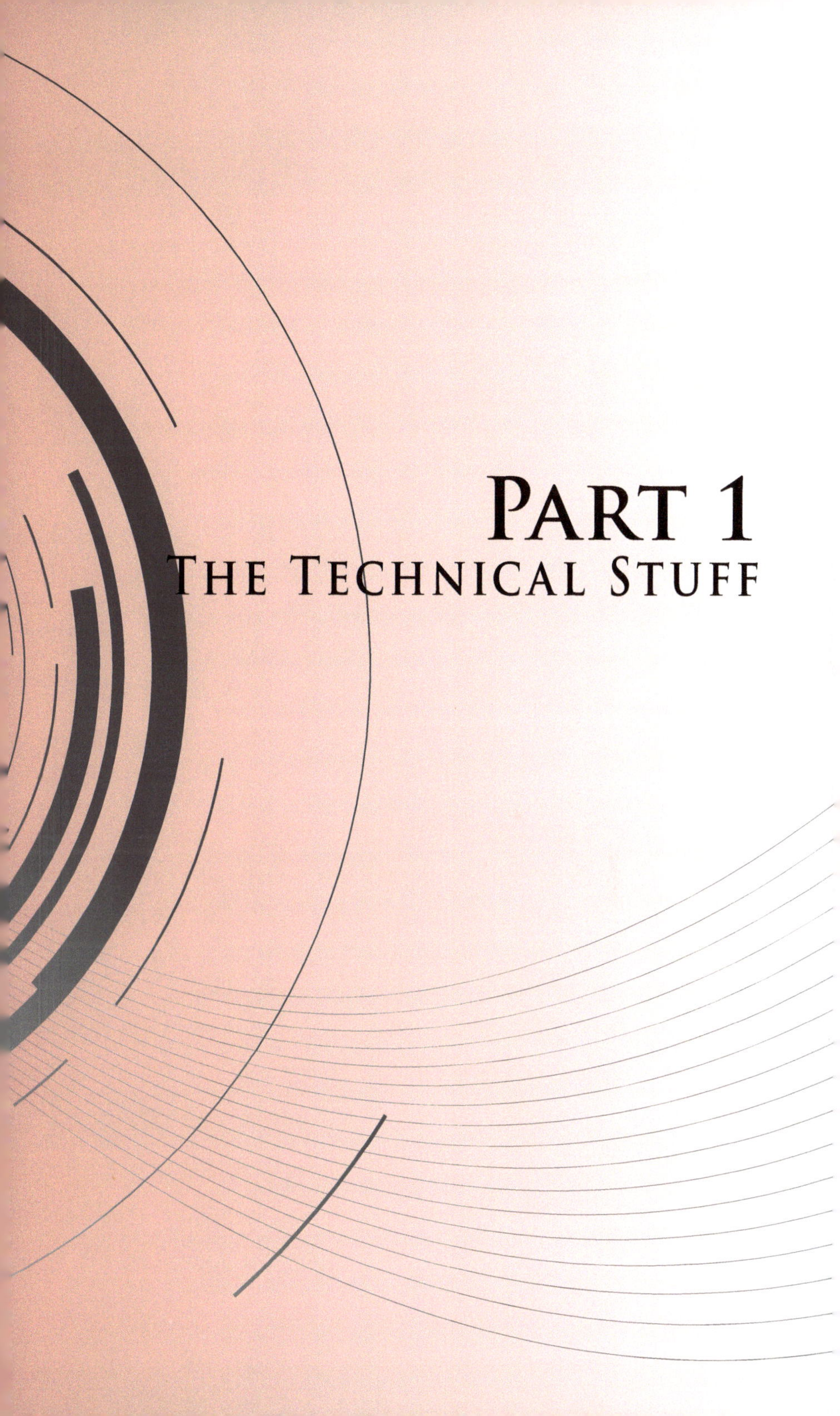
PART 1
THE TECHNICAL STUFF

To start with, we need to learn the concepts of the science of photography, the technical stuff that most of us don't want to get into too deeply. However, without a basic understanding of these concepts, it will be difficult to improve your photography. Why do you need to have this understanding? Because the automatic modes of a DSLR don't always make the choices that we want for our images. You need to be familiar with the features and functions of the camera so you can take control and create the image you want.

UNDERSTANDING YOUR CAMERA AND ITS SETTINGS

The best way to understand what all of those buttons and dials on your camera mean is to read the manual. It may not make a lot of sense in the beginning, but as you move through this book, you'll begin to put it together and you may even surprise yourself by picking up some very good ideas on how to use the functions of your camera to create interesting images.

PARTS OF THE CAMERA

It's called a single lens reflex camera because a single lens, the one on the front of the camera, is used to create the image. The light coming through this lens is also reflected up thru the pentaprism to the viewfinder. Let's look at the major parts of a DSLR.

The major parts of the camera are:

1 Interchangeable lens and aperture

2 Mirror

3 Focal plane shutter (shutter)

4 Sensor or film

5 Focusing screen

6 Condensing lens

7 Pentaprism

8 Viewfinder eyepiece

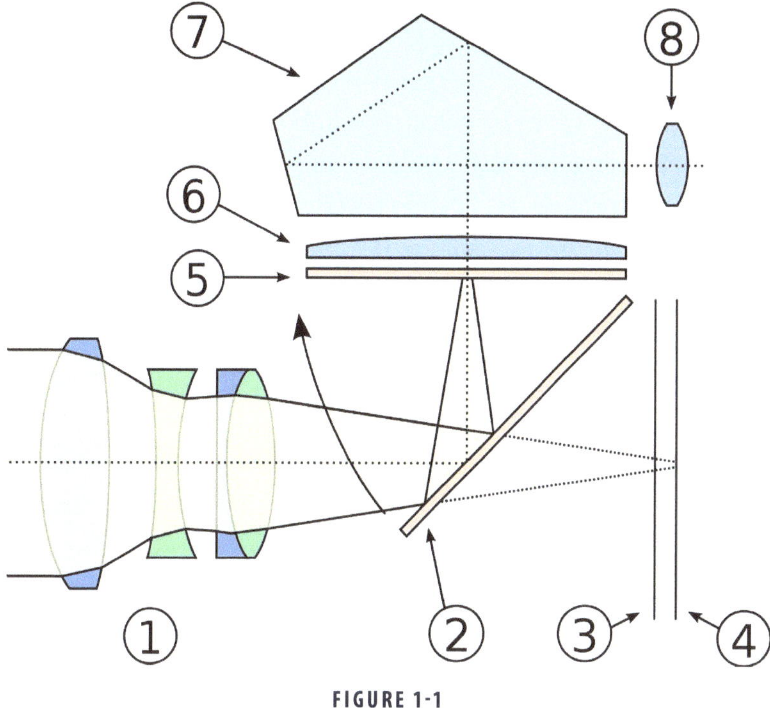

FIGURE 1-1

A cross-section of the optical components of a typical digital or film SLR camera shows how the light passes through the lens and aperture assembly **(1)**, is reflected by the mirror **(2)** and is projected on the matte focusing screen **(5)**. Via a condensing lens **(6)** and internal reflections in the roof pentaprism **(7)** the image appears in the eyepiece **(8)**. When an image is taken, the mirror moves upwards from its critical 45 degree angle in the direction of the arrow, the focal plane shutter **(3)** opens, and the image is projected onto the sensor or film **(4)** in exactly the same manner as on the focusing screen.

SENSOR SIZE AND CROP FACTOR

There are many different types and sizes of sensors used in digital photography. In 35mm digital photography the most popular sensor types are CMOS (Complementary Metal Oxide Semiconductor) and CCD (Charge Coupled Device). Discussions of these technologies are outside the scope of this book, but suffice it to say, both technologies create the image without the photographer having to do anything with them.

The sensor size (Figure 1-2) and how it affects the image, is something of which the photographer should at least have an understanding. There are two main sensor sizes used in 35mm photography. Most consumer cameras use the APS-C (15mm x 22.5mm) crop sensor. Professional or pro-consumer cameras may have a full frame (36mm x24mm) sensor or a sensor that is the same size as a frame of 35mm film. A crop sensor camera, one that uses an APS-C sensor, will not show as much of the frame as a full frame sensor. This difference is called the crop factor.

The crop factor in Canon APS-C cameras is 1.6 and in Nikon APS-C cameras is 1.5. Essentially the crop factor creates images that seem closer or have the effect of using a longer focal length lens. To calculate the effective focal length any lens on a camera with a crop factor sensor, multiply the crop factor by the lens focal length to get the effective focal length of the lens. The focal length of a lens is defined as the distance from the center of a lens to the point where the image is in focus. This will be discussed more in Part 2: Lenses.[1]

Figure 1-3 shows the effect that an APS-C sensor (blue rectangle) has on the image as compared to a full frame sensor (red rectangle). A crop sensor effectively changes the field of view of the lens by the crop factor.

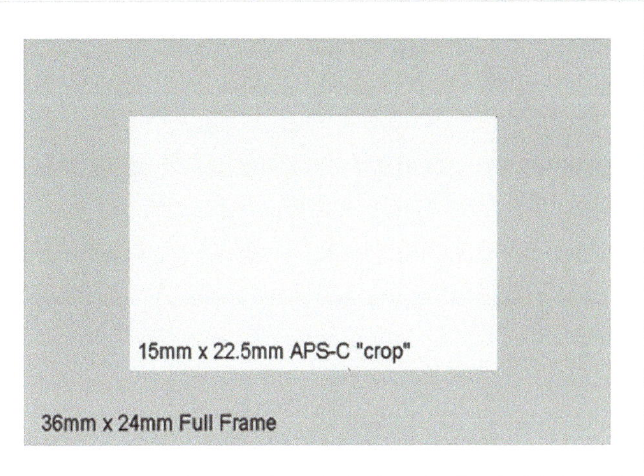

[1]**FIGURE 1-2**

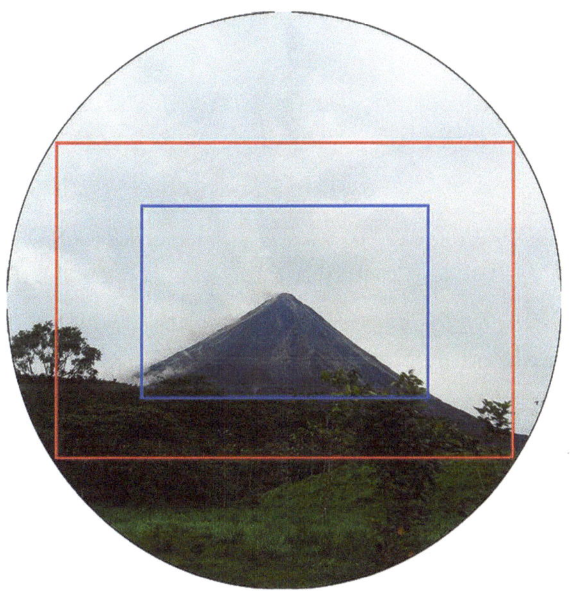

[2]**FIGURE 1-3**

---

[1] Wikipedia Creative Commons license
[2] Wikipedia Creative Commons license

Camera Dials and Buttons

Most digital cameras have a set of common modes for picture taking. (Be sure to refer to the manual for your camera for an explanation of the specific dials and buttons.) There is the Full Auto mode where the camera acts like a point and shoot camera. Then there is the semi-automatic or Basic Zone, the Creative Zone and finally, there is the full manual mode.

In the Basic Zones, the camera makes most, if not all, of the choices when you press the shutter. These zones include, but aren't limited to, Portrait, Landscape, Close-up, Sports, etc. In these modes, the camera is programmed to certain settings for specific types of images. You may have the ability to shift the settings, but you are shifting all of the settings. These can be useful while you gain experience and before you start using the Creative Zones.

The Creative Zones include, but aren't limited to, Shutter Priority, Aperture Priority, Manual, etc. In these zones, you can choose what value to use and the camera will choose the other. In Shutter Priority for example, you choose the shutter speed and depending on the amount of light the camera meter reads, it would choose the aperture to create a properly exposed image. In Aperture Priority mode, you choose the aperture and the camera chooses the shutter speed.

In Manual Mode, you, the photographer, have full control over the settings of the camera. You may use settings that would over or under expose the image and the camera will not make any changes to them. Manual mode is where your vision of the image can be created without the input of the camera.

Changing the Lens

Because the sensor is susceptible to collecting dust, it's advisable to change the lens as quickly as possible. A good way of doing this is as follows:

1   Power the camera off (helps prevent dust from accumulating on the sensor)

2   Point the camera down and, if outside, turn your back to the wind.

3   Press the lens lock release and:

    a   Twist the lens till it stops

    b   Remove the lens and cover the rear element

    c   Line up the dots of the new lens and camera body

    d   Twist in the opposite direction as before until it locks.

By performing this procedure as quickly as possible, you will minimize dust collecting opportunities, keep it clean longer and prevent those spots and blotches that will show on your images when the sensor is dirty.

Holding the Camera

Properly supporting a DSLR provides the photographer with a steady base to create sharp images. Often folks that have a camera with an EVF (electronic view finder that uses the LCD (Liquid Crystal Display) on the back of the camera as the viewfinder) hold it at arm's length to take the picture. This just about guarantees blurry images caused by camera shake. To prevent blur from camera motion, practice these techniques:

Use a tripod. Although they aren't always convenient to carry around, they are the best way to make sure the camera is steady. Another option is to put your camera on a table, rock, fence or some other object to support it.

What if you don't have one? Do what the person is doing in Figure 1-4; she is making herself the tripod for the camera. She's supporting the camera and lens with her left hand, holding the body of it with her right hand and putting her index finger just above the shutter release button, ready to squeeze off a shot. Additional stability is provided for the camera as she rests her elbows on her knees.

When standing, have your feet about shoulder width apart, one foot slightly in front of the other and pull your elbows in toward your stomach/chest. This recreates the legs of a tripod and creates a great foundation from which to start your image. You may even want to lean against something solid, providing further stability to you and the camera.

This technique can be used with any type of camera, whether it uses an LCD as the viewfinder or a pentaprism like a DSLR.

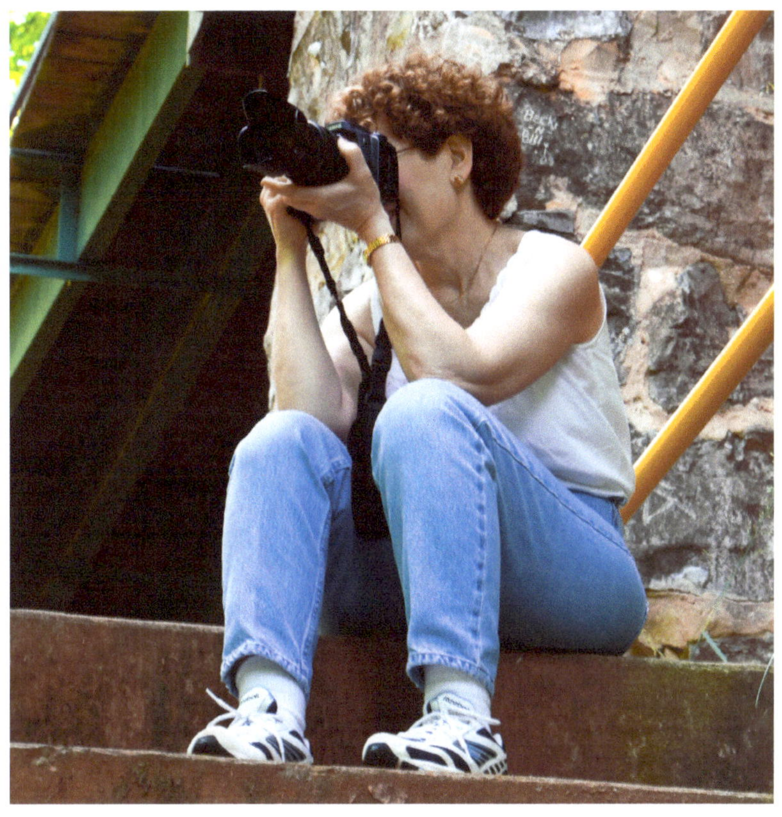

FIGURE 1-4

FOCUSING THE CAMERA

There are two way to focus your camera, manual and auto. In manual mode, you turn the focus ring on the lens until the image in the viewfinder is in focus. This method gives you total creative control on where you want the viewer to look by placing only that area in focus. With today's DSLR's, this is sometimes difficult to achieve because there are no helper items like a split prism in the viewfinder to assist you in focusing.

In auto mode, when you press the shutter button half way down, the camera uses the built-in focus points (the small rectangles in Figure 1-5) to find a high contrast area and then focus on that point. This sometimes results in the wrong things being in focus because the camera really doesn't know where you want the focus point to be.

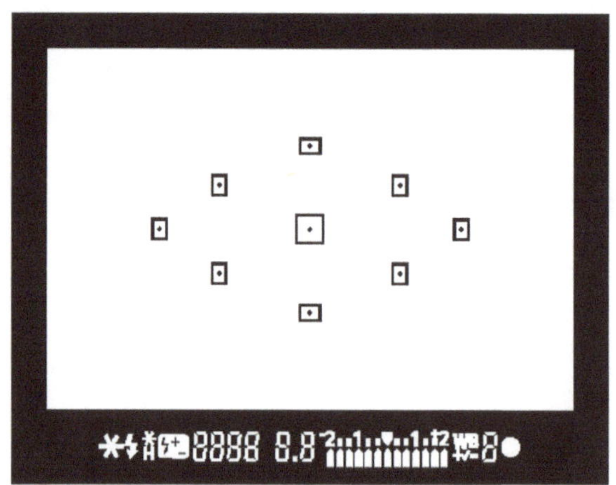

Viewfinder

FIGURE 1-5

One way around this is to manually set which focus point the camera will use. This is usually done by a selector button on the back of the camera and allows you to choose any of the available focus points.

Some DSLR's allow the user to move the focus function away from the shutter button. This is useful because the first thing a DSLR does when you press the shutter button is to calculate the exposure setting and select the focus point. Isolating the focus function away from the exposure function allows you to focus on a particular point and then use your creativity to recompose the image and maintain the focus on the point you chose, giving you more creative control of the imaging process.

Squeeze the Shutter

Blurry pictures can still happen even if you're holding the camera as described in the previous section if you jerk your finger on the shutter button to take the image. Nine times out of 10, by jerking your finger on the shutter button, you will move the camera just when it needs to be its most steady. It's better to squeeze the shutter button and be surprised when it goes off rather than to jerk your finger on the button and move the camera.

Proper Breathing

The way you breathe when taking images will affect your steadiness also. Here is an easily learned technique. First take a few deep breaths in and let them out slowly. When you're ready to take the picture, take in one more deep breath, let it out slowly and hold your breath when you empty your lungs. This will create a few seconds of stillness in your body, you'll be relaxed, and you can gently squeeze the shutter button without affecting the stability of the camera.

THE EXPOSURE TRIANGLE

The exposure triangle (Figure 1-6) shows the relationship between shutter speed, aperture and ISO. Every image is made up of the combination of a certain shutter speed, at a certain aperture, with a certain ISO. These are the ingredients for a photographic recipe.

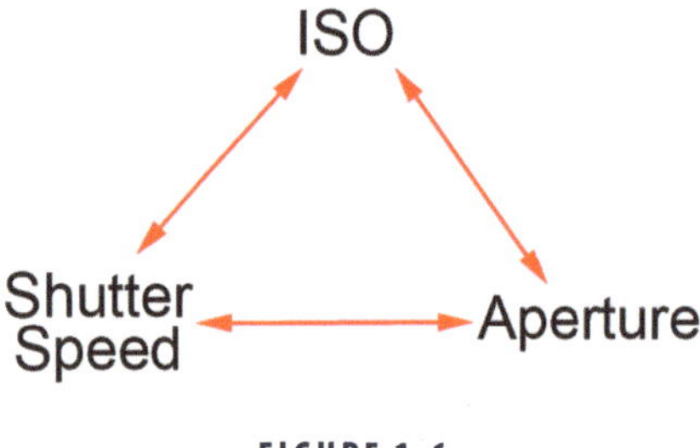

FIGURE 1-6

In order to produce the same image time after time, you need to adhere to this recipe. If you modify one of the ingredients, you need to modify one or both of the other ingredients in order to produce the same result.

If you open the aperture by one stop, in order to obtain the same image as before, you need to shorten the shutter speed by one stop or lower the ISO by the same one stop amount. This will ensure that the photographic recipe will produce the same results.

This is also called the law of reciprocity. For a given exposure, if you change the shutter speed, you must reciprocate and change the aperture or the ISO by the same amount, but in the opposite direction, to obtain the same given exposure.

ISO OR ASA OR DIN

ISO is the International Standards Organization, a body that runs tests and creates standards to determine a film's or sensor's sensitivity to light. When referencing film, there can be two other acronyms, ASA and DIN. ASA stands for the American Standards Association and DIN stands for Deutches Institut fur Normung. Both are organizations that create standards used to determine a film's sensitivity to light.

ISO is the acronym used today for determining the sensitivity of the sensor or film. The higher number denotes more sensitivity to light and it can range from ISO 6 to ISO 102,400. The higher sensitivities are more susceptible to sensor noise for digital cameras or will have larger film grain. (Grain is the light sensitive bits of the film.) Today's cameras often can attain an ISO setting of 25,600 but the amount of noise from the amplifiers in the sensor may be unacceptable for your images.

THE SHUTTER

The shutter allows light to fall on the camera's sensor for a specific amount of time. Common shutter speeds are from 1/4000th of a second to 30 seconds. Some cameras expand this to 1/8000th of a second on the fast end and to 'B' or Bulb on slow end. The term Bulb goes back to the time when cameras had a pneumatically controlled shutter with an air filled rubber bulb. You would squeeze the bulb to open the shutter and it would stay open until you released the bulb. Today it just means the shutter will stay open as long as the photographer holds the shutter button down. It is used to create exposures longer than the camera is designed to do automatically.

Today's shutters usually contain two curtains or blades that chase one another across the sensor to allow the required amount of light in.

1
Viewfinder view
2
Shutter Cocked
3
1st blade starts
4
2nd blade starts
5
6
7
Blades continue the chase across the frame
8
Shutter closed

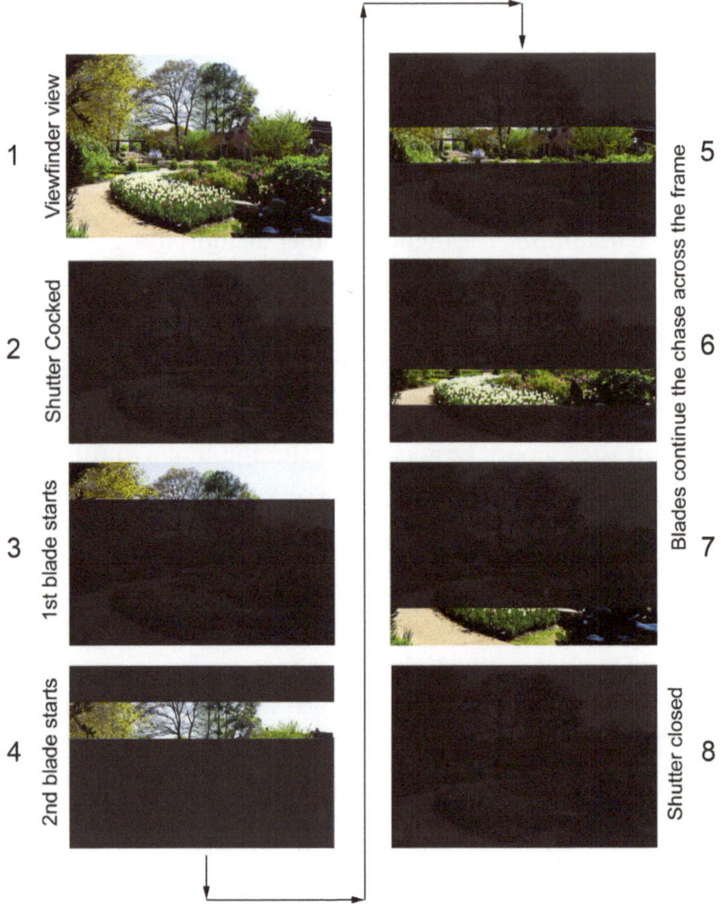

FIGURE 1-7

The sequence of images in Figure 1-7 demonstrates the shutter operation at 1/1000th of a second. (1) The viewfinder presents the full image. When the shutter is pressed (2), the first curtain/blade that was cocked is released. (3) 1/1000th of a second later the second curtain/blade is released and chases the first across the sensor, creating a slot whose duration is the selected shutter speed until it is fully closed (4-8). The longer the shutter speed, the wider the slot becomes until the first becomes fully open before the second starts to close.

APERTURE

The aperture, the maximum opening of the lens, is synonymous with the term f-stop and it controls the amount of light that enters the lens. It can be set manually by the photographer or automatically set by the camera. The aperture number, called the f-number, is the ratio of the lens' focal length divided by the size of the opening at the back of the lens. For example, a lens with a 100mm focal length that has a 25mm opening at the back of the lens has a maximum aperture of f/4.0. Because the f-number is a ratio, an aperture of f/5.6 on a 50mm lens lets in the same about of light that an aperture of f/5.6 on a 200mm lens does.

Mechanical blades inside the lens create apertures or openings other than the maximum aperture of the lens. Figure 1-8 shows that as the number in the aperture or f-stop gets larger, the size of the opening gets smaller. For example, the size or area of the aperture opening at f/16 is eight times smaller than the size or area of the aperture opening when set at f/2, letting in eight times less light than the f/2 aperture.

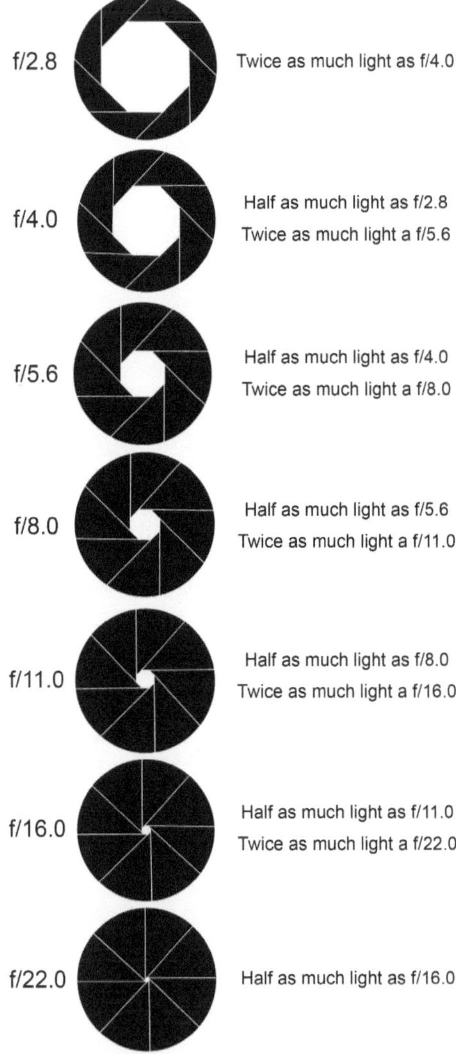

Some lens barrels do not display the aperture markings on them or have the ability to set the aperture by twisting a ring on the lens barrell. Instead the f-stops are set by dials or menus on the camera.

FIGURE 1-8

The maximum aperture a lens can obtain also determines what is called lens speed. For example, an f/2.8 lens is faster than an f/5.6 lens, because it lets in more light so you can use a faster shutter speed to obtain the same exposure of an image.

SHUTTER SPEED – LENGTH OF TIME LIGHT IS LET IN

Different effects can be obtained by varying shutter speed. The images in Figure 1-9 were shot 15 minutes after sundown and show the effect the shutter speed has on an image while using a constant aperture. Slower shutter speeds let light in for a longer period of time, creating a brighter image.

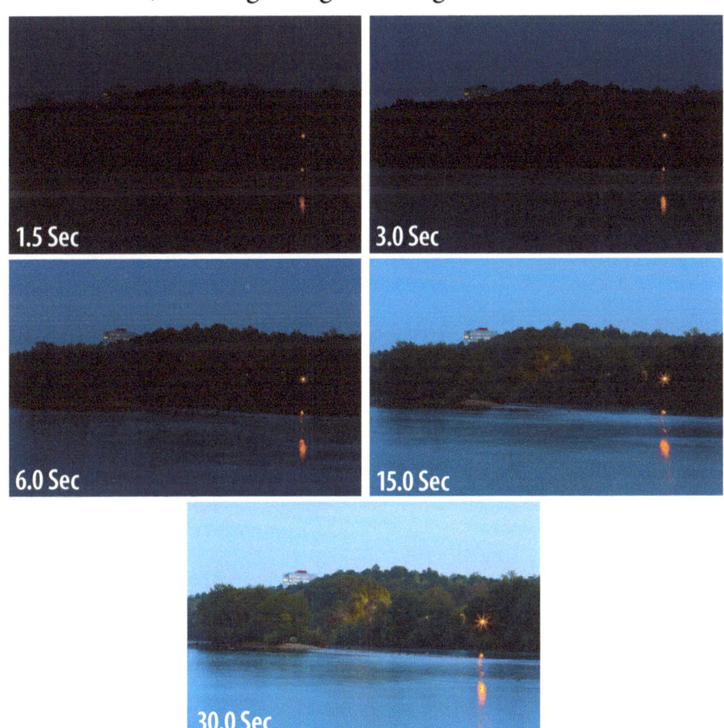

FIGURE 1-9

SHUTTER SPEED CONTROLS MOTION

Figure 1-10 thru 1-12 demonstrate the effects that different shutter speeds and apertures have on an image.

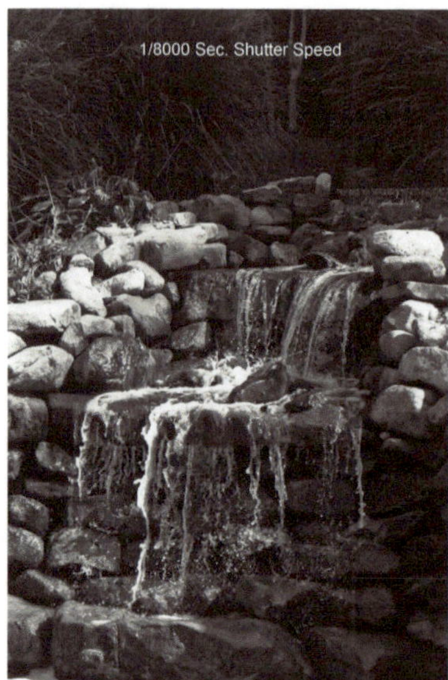

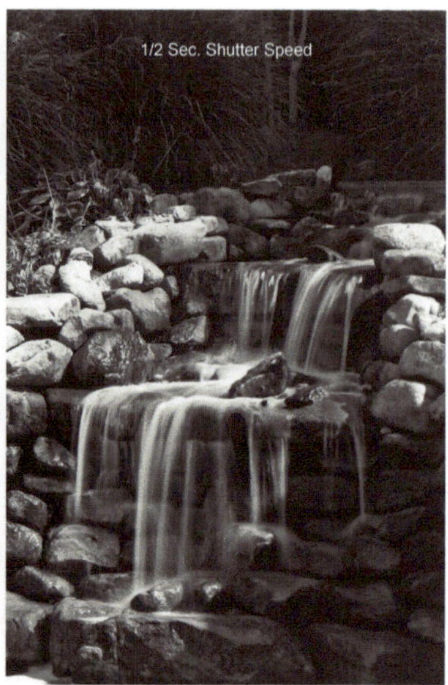

FIGURE 1-10

In figure 1-10 to freeze the waterfall use a fast shutter speed. To create a silky smooth waterfall, use a slow shutter speed. You may also need to add neutral density filters to the lens to reduce the amount of light coming in to the camera so that you can use a shutter speed slow enough to create the silky water effect.

Shutter Speed – Creates Motion

To create motion in a still image, use a tripod and a relatively slow shutter speed. Figure 1-11 shows vehicles accelerating from a stop light. The effect in Figure 1-11 is created because the distance from the camera to the vehicles determines how fast they appear to be moving. Vehicles that are further away appear slower while closer vehicles appear to be moving very fast.

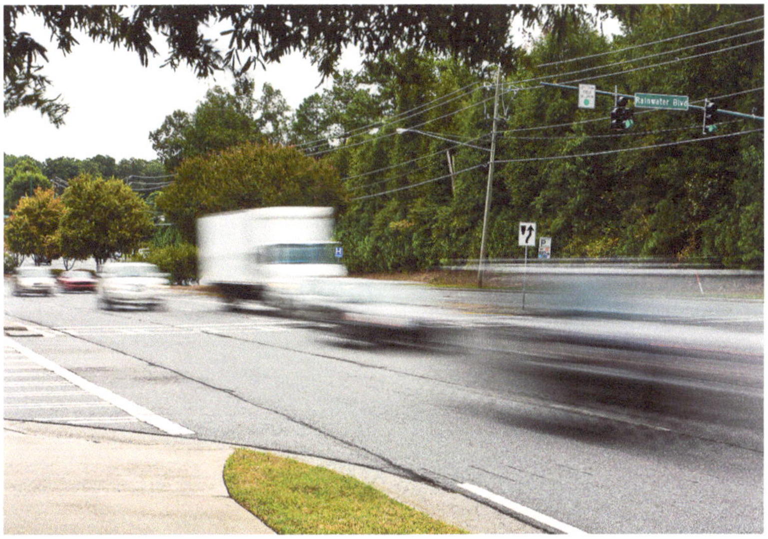

FIGURE 1-11

APERTURE EFFECTS

The background effects demonstrated in Figure 1-12 are created by changing the aperture of the lens. The smaller the aperture that is chosen, the larger the depth of field becomes in the image (For more on depth of field see Part 2.) and the sharper the background appears behind the subject. This can lead the viewer to concentrate on the background instead of the subject. By using a wide aperture, the subject is isolated preventing the viewer from concentrating on the background and keeping their attention on the subject.

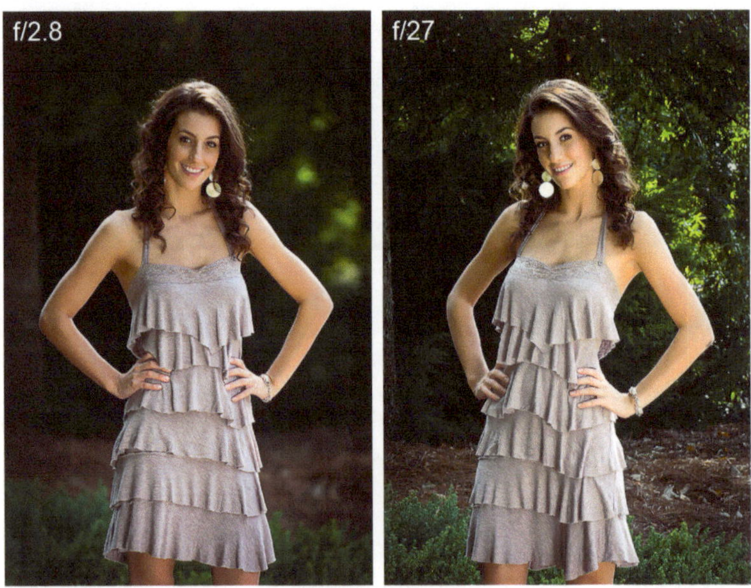

FIGURE 1-12

Photographic Stop

The halving or doubling of light entering the camera is called a stop. For example, changing your shutter speed from 1/2000s to 1/1000s is doubling the amount of light let in while the shutter is open and is opening up one stop. Changing your shutter from f/8 to f/11 is halving the amount of light let in through the lens and is closing down one stop. And changing your ISO from 200 to 400 is doubling the sensors sensitivity to light and is opening up one stop.

The charts in Figure 1-13 show the values for shutter speed and aperture camera manufacturers use as standard settings. If the camera is set to make changes in full stop increments, the settings under the 'FULL' columns will be seen. Half stop increments will see the settings under '1/2' and for third stop increments the settings under '1/3' will be seen. This of course is manufacturer dependent and they may not include all settings.

To change the exposure by 2 stops, determine if Full, 1/2 or 1/3 increments are used in the camera and then move the dial in the correct direction, by 2, 4 or 6 steps respectively.

As an example, in manual mode, if an ISO of 100 and a shutter speed of 1/1000 second at an aperture of f/8 is used, to open up 2 stops changing only the shutter, move the shutter speed dial until it displays 1/250 second.

Shutter Speed Stop Guide					
Full	1/2		1/3		
4000	4000	8	4000	60	1"
2000	3000	6	3200	50	1"3
1000	2000	4	2500	40	1"6
500	1500	0"3	2000	30	2"
250	1000	0"5	1600	25	2"5
125	750	0"7	1250	20	3"2
60	500	1"	1000	15	4"
30	350	1"5	800	13	5"
15	250	2"	640	10	6"
8	180	3"	500	8	8"
4	125	4"	400	6	10"
0"5	90	6"	320	5	13"
1"	60	8"	250	4	15"
2"	45	10"	200	0"3	20"
4"	30	15"	160	0"4	25"
8"	20	20"	125	0"5	30"
15"	15	30"	100	0"6	
30"	10		80	0"8	

Aperture f-Stop Guide					
Full	1/2		1/3		
f-1	f-1	f-13	f-1	f-5.6	f-32
f-1.4	f-1.2	f-16	f-1.1	f-6.3	f-36
f-2	f-1.4	f-19	f-1.2	f-7.1	f-40
f-2.8	f-1.8	f-22	f-1.4	f-8	f-45
f-4	f-2	f-27	f-1.6	f-9	f-51
f-5.6	f-2.5	f-32	f-1.8	f-10	f-57
f-8	f-2.8	f-38	f-2	f-11	f-64
f-11	f-3.5	f-45	f-2.2	f-13	f-72
f-16	f-4	f-54	f-2.5	f-14	f-81
f-22	f-4.5	f-64	f-2.8	f-16	f-91
f-32	f-5.6	f-76	f-3.2	f-18	f-101
f-45	f-6.7	f-91	f-3.5	f-20	f-113
f-64	f-8		f-4	f-22	f-128
f-90	f-9.5		f-4.5	f-25	
f-128	f-11		f-5	f-29	

FIGURE 1-13

Exposure Value (EV)

In photography, exposure value (EV) denotes all combinations of a camera's shutter speed and relative aperture that give the same exposure at the same ISO.

For example, if the camera settings of 100 ISO with an aperture of f/4 and a shutter speed of 1/60th is an EV of 10, then the camera settings of ISO of 100 with an aperture of f/8 and a shutter speed of 1/15th will also be an EV of 10.

White Balance

In a digital camera, white balance is what makes white look white. Back in the film days, a different kind of film was used depending on what light you were shooting under. Normal indoor lighting is usually created by tungsten elements in the light bulbs so to prevent the image from having an orange or yellowish cast to it, an indoor or tungsten balanced film was used versus daylight balanced film that was used for outdoor photography.

With digital cameras, either an 'Auto White Balance' is set or the camera's white balance is changed to one of the many settings it has (i.e. Shady, Tungsten, Cloudy, Daylight...etc.) in order to create or remove an overall color cast on your image. Some camera's have the ability to set color temperature directly by setting a specific Kelvin temperature. The chart in Figure 1-14 shows the Kelvin temperature of the different kinds of light sources.

Color Temperature	
1000K	Candles; oil lamps
2000K	Very early sunrise; low effect tungsten lamps
2500K	Household light bulbs
3000K	Studio lights, photo floods
4000K	Clear flashbulbs - what are they?
5000K	Typical daylight; electronic flash
5500K	The sun at noon near Kodak's offices
6000K	Bright sunshine with clear sky
7000K	Slightly overcast sky
8000K	Hazy sky
9000K	Open shade on clear day
10000K	Heavily overcast sky
11000K	Sunless blue skies
20000+K	Open shade in mountains on a really clear day

FIGURE 1-14

The images in figure 1-15 show the effect that white balance has on an image taken under normal daylight conditions. As you can see, by changing the white balance setting on the camera, very creative effects can be applied to the images.

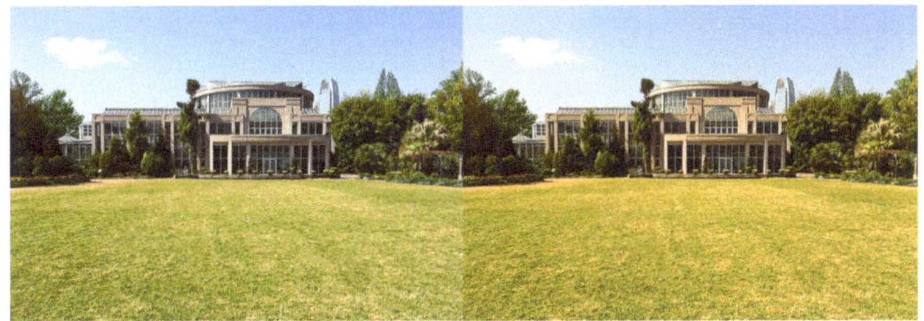

Daylight White BalanceCloudy White Balance

Daylight White Balance   Cloudy White Balance

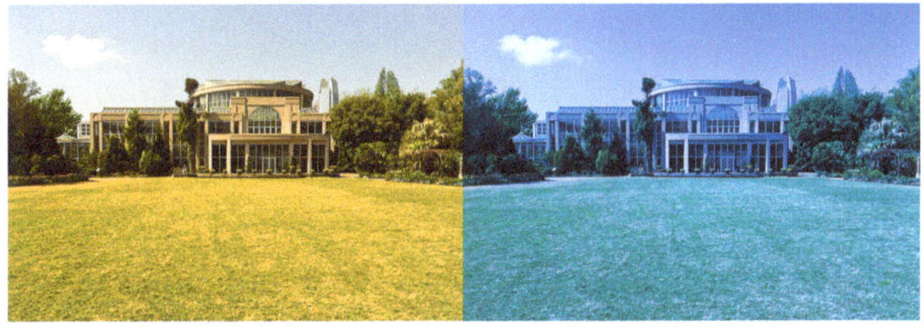

Shade White Balance   Tungsten White Balance

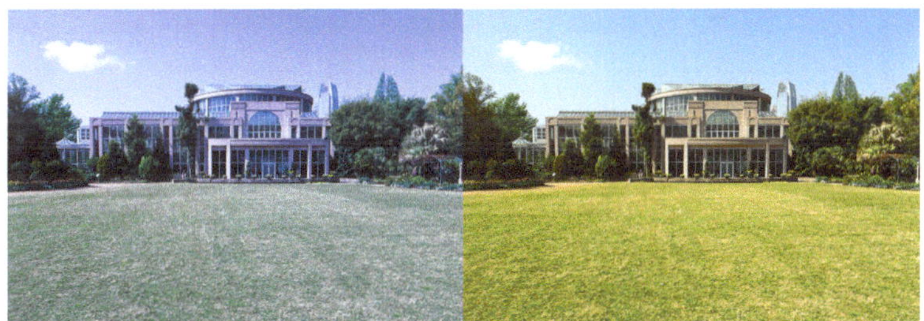

Flourescent White Balance   Flash White Balance

FIGURE 1-15

METERING

A light meter is a device that measures the amount of light, in photographic terms, falling on or being reflected from a scene. It then gives the photographer an educated decision on what a good exposure should be. Metering devices are either external hand held devices or are built into the body of the camera. They are calibrated to make everything 'middle' or 18% grey. In other words, if you meter a white wall, the exposure the meter will tell you, will produce an image of the wall that looks like it is middle or 18% grey. In photography, middle grey is a tone that is perceptually about half way between black and white on a lightness scale and in photography, it is typically defined as 18% reflectance in visible light. You can purchase a grey card (Figure 1-16) at a photo store and use it to determine exposure.

FIGURE 1-16

18% Grey Card

There are two types of light meters, incident and reflected. An incident light meter, measures the amount of light that is falling on a scene. A reflected light meter, measures the amount of light that is reflected from a scene.

Hand held meters (Figure 1-17) can be either incident, or reflected light meters, or both. All in-camera light meters are reflected light meters because the camera is seeing light that is reflected from the scene.

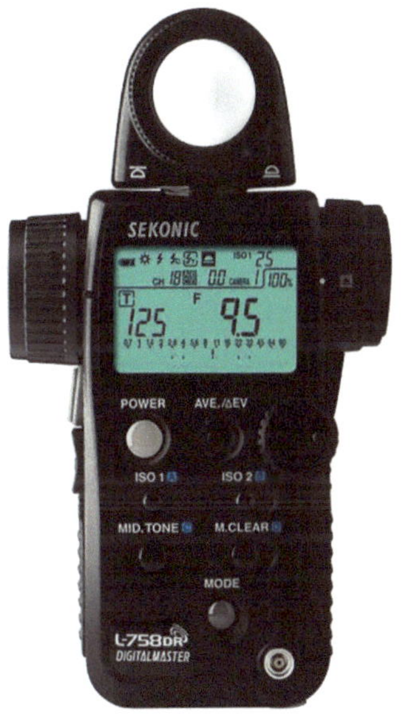

FIGURE 1-17

A Sekonic 758 is a hand held light meter that is both
an incident as well as a reflected light meter.

The camera's internal light meter has 3-4 metering modes. Depending on the manufacturer and camera model, the modes are called different names, but their concepts are essentially the same. In a Canon camera, they are usually called Evaluative, Partial, Spot, and Center Weighted Average. For Nikon, they can be called 3D Color Matrix Metering II, Center-weighted and Spot.

The calculations the camera meter makes are based on the selected metering mode. In Canon cameras for example, Evaluative metering, the camera's viewfinder is divided into zones and the meter then evaluates the amount of light coming from each zone to determine a proper overall exposure. Partial metering, normally used when the backgrounds are brighter than the subject, looks at roughly 8% of the view finder area to determine exposure. Spot metering looks at 3.5% of the viewfinder area to determine exposure and Center-Weighted Average metering is weighted toward the center of the viewfinder and then averaged for the entire scene to determine exposure.

Nikon 3D Color Matrix Metering II mode meters a wide area of the frame and sets the exposure according to a distribution of the brightness. Center Weighted meters the entire frame and assigns a greater weight to the center area of the frame to determine exposure. Spot metering uses a 3.5mm circle in the center of the frame to determine the exposure.

With today's DSLR's you have the ability to change the metering mode on every image to help insure proper exposure.

RAW OR JPEG

Digital cameras today capture the image as an electronic file. There are two different file types that can be used to capture the image: RAW and JPEG. The user determines whether the camera will create RAW, JPEG, or both, by making choices on the camera's menu.

RAW – It is essentially the digital negative. Each camera creates a RAW file when the data is captured from the camera's sensor. This is a proprietary format that requires special software that is usually provided by the manufacturer, to create a final image. Programs like Photoshop or Photoshop Elements also read the RAW data to create the image on the computer. RAW format is not compressed to save space.

JPEG is a standardized image file format that uses compression algorithms to save storage space. The compression algorithms actually remove data from the RAW format to create that smaller file.

di Sogno
PHOTOGRAPHY

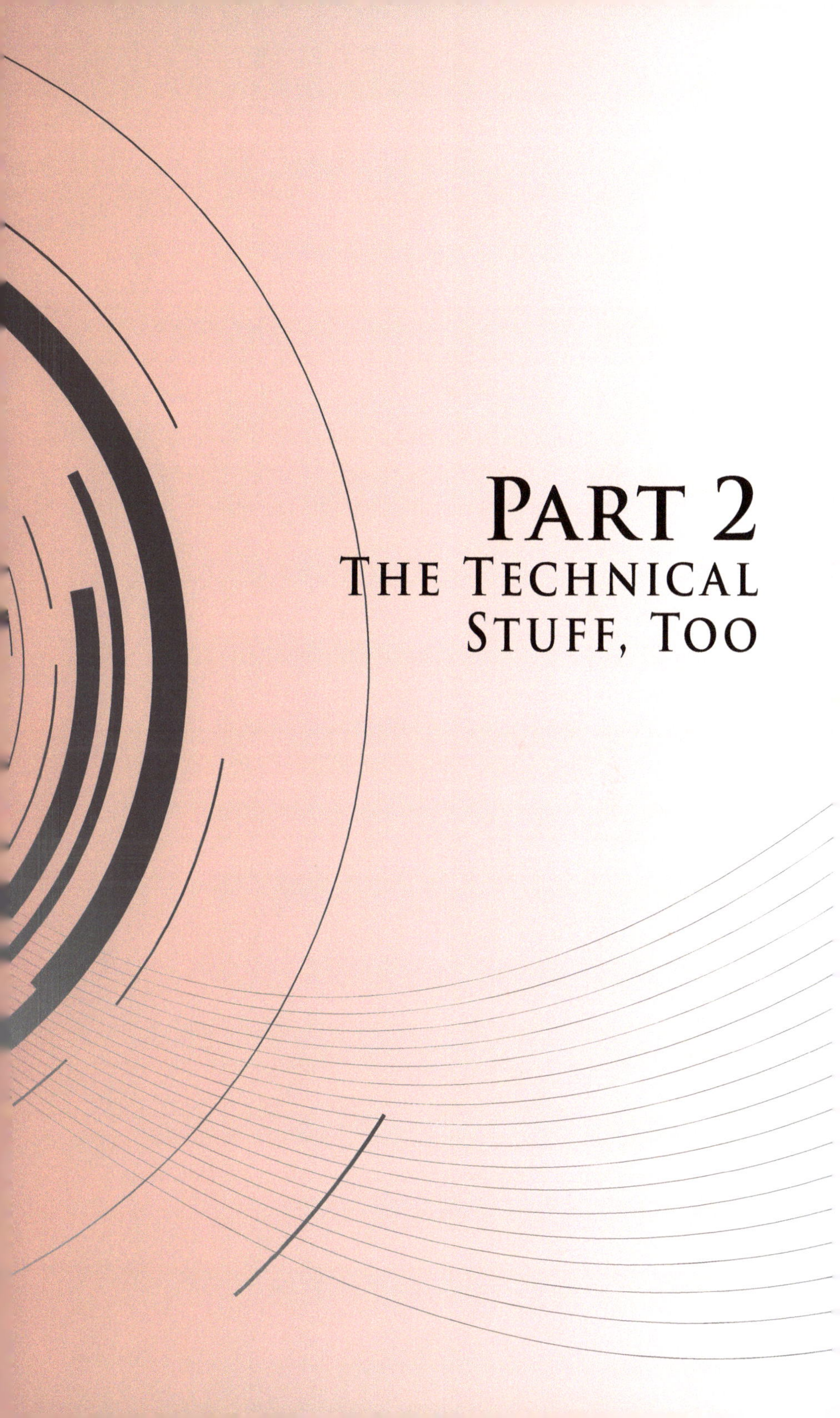

PART 2
THE TECHNICAL STUFF, TOO

LENSES

Once you have a basic understanding of your camera controls it's time to look at the different effects and perspectives that changing your lens will have on the composition of your images. For example a telephoto lens will allow you to fill the frame with your subject from a far distance or a wide angle lens will allow you to create photos that can seem surreal. A telephoto lens can compress the image and throw the background out of focus. A wide angle lens will distort images and can make a person's nose seem extra large. There are even lenses that can fix converging lines in images of buildings.

Lenses come in all shapes and sizes, from ultra wide lenses to super telephoto lenses. They are available in a fixed or variable focal length and have either a fixed or variable aperture. You will more than likely use lens in the wide, standard or telephoto category with a fixed or variable focal length. A fixed focal length lens is called a prime lens and a variable focal length lens is called a zoom lens.

The focal length of a lens is defined as the distance from the center of a lens to the point where the image is in focus. The camera's sensor or film is found at this point.

A standard lens, so called because it gives a field of view roughly equal to what the human eye sees, is normally made with a focal length between 45-55mm on a standard full frame 35mm camera. Wide angle lenses have a field of view greater than what the human eye sees and are defined by a focal length of less than 40mm. Some of the more common sizes are 24mm, 28mm and 35mm focal lengths. Telephoto lenses give a field of view that is narrower than what the human eye sees and they begin at 60mm and longer.

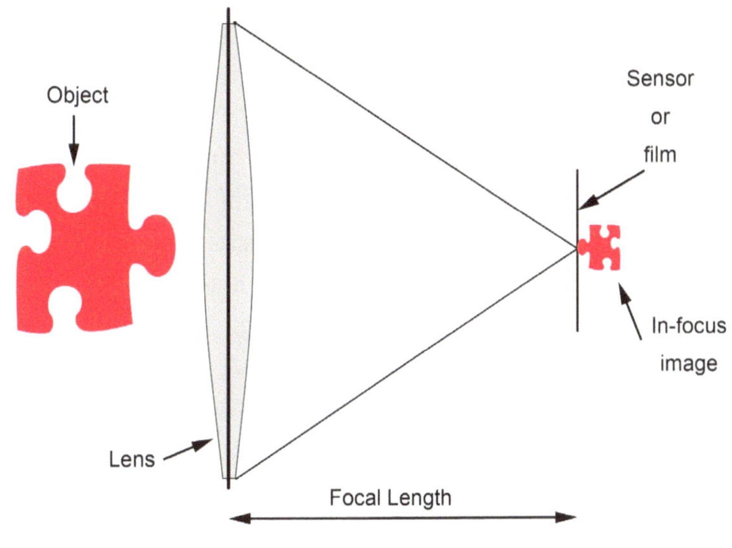

FIGURE 2-1

Determining Focal Length

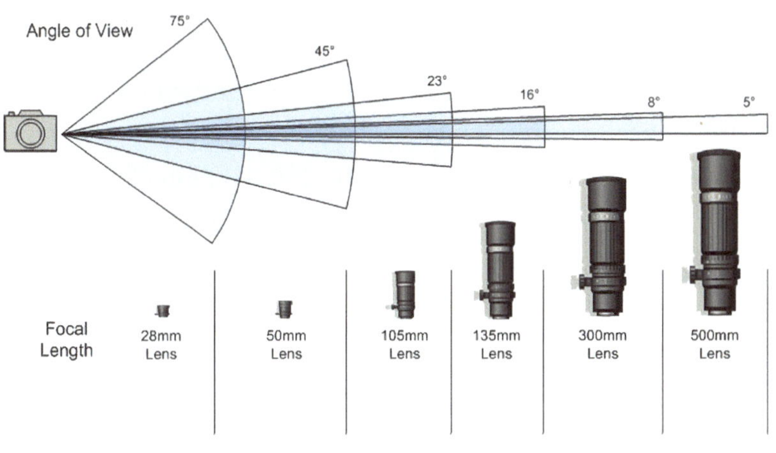

FIGURE 2-2

*The field of view for the most common fixed
focal length lenses used on a 35mm DSLR*

Zoom lenses combine different focal lengths into a single lens. A popular size for a wide to short telephoto lens is a 28-135mm focal length. Most consumer zooms have a variable maximum aperture instead of a fixed maximum aperture. This means, that as the focal length gets longer, the maximum aperture of the lens gets smaller. The 28-135mm lens above has a variable aperture of f3.5-5.6. At the 28mm end, the maximum aperture of the lens is f3.5 and at 135mm end it has changed to f5.6.

A term you've probably heard is lens speed. A lens's speed is determined by the maximum aperture that lens can obtain. A 'fast' lens is one with a maximum aperture of f2.8 or larger and a 'slow' lens has a maximum aperture of above f3.5. So the above lens is a medium to slow lens because its maximum aperture starts at f3.5 and slows to f5.6 as the focal length increases.

A very useful side effect of wide angle lenses is that they produce images with a large depth of field when compared to a normal lens at the same aperture. This means that much more of the image will be sharp and makes them more useful in low light situations where you may not be able to fine tune your focus prior to clicking the shutter.

A byproduct of depth of field is the blurred or out of focus area of an image. The term used to describe the esthetic quality of the blur is Bokeh. Lens design, focal length and the number of blades in the aperture all have an effect on Bokeh.

Telephoto lenses have just the opposite effect; they compress the image and have a much shorter depth of field when compared to a normal lens at the same aperture. Image compression is effectively moving distant objects in the image so that they look like they are close to the subject. You've seen this effect in images made at a football game with the super telephoto lenses used by sports photographers.

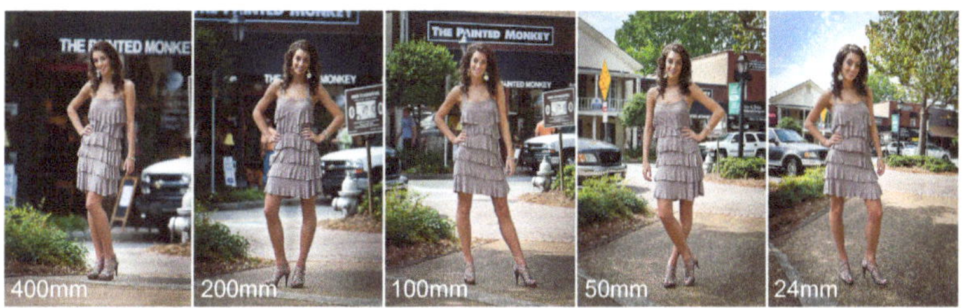

FIGURE 2-3

The visual perspective of a lens allows different effects to be created. In Figure 2-3, at a focal length of 400mm the background is compressed and it appears as though the model is standing directly in front of the shop. As the focal length decreases, the compression decreases, and at a focal length of 24mm it seems as though the model is a long way from the shops. A standard 50mm focal length the perspective is one with which we are all familiar because that is what we see with the naked eye.

DEPTH OF FIELD

Depth of field is the distance between the nearest and the farthest objects that are acceptably sharp. That acceptably sharp distance extends from 1/3rd of the focus distance in front, to 2/3rds of the focus distance behind the focus point.

The example shown in Figure 2-4 is using f/11 as the aperture, with the focus point at 10 feet in front of the camera, any item that is 1/3rd of that distance in front of the focus point to approximately 2/3rds of that distance behind the focus point will be in focus. That works out to be 10-(10*.3) = 7 ft. in front to 10+(10*.6) = 16 ft. will be in focus. The DOF is approximately 9 feet.

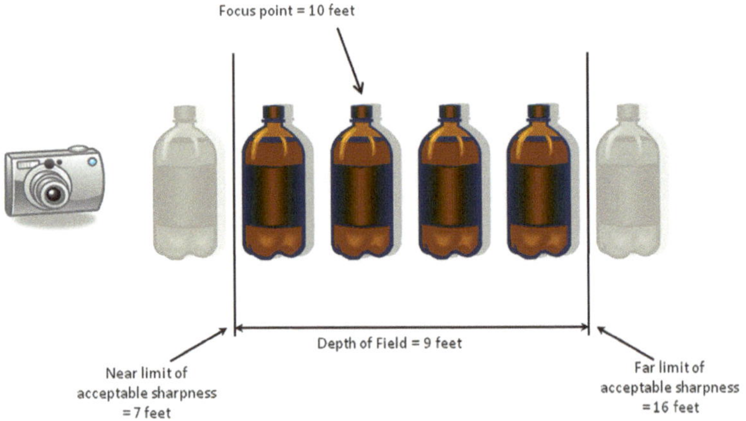

FIGURE 2-4

Of course this is a simplification. In reality, the camera's sensor size, the aperture, the focal length and the subject to camera distance all go into calculating the DOF.

DOF can be summed up like this:

- As the camera to the subject distance increases, DOF increases.

- As the aperture f-stop increases, DOF increases.

- As the lens focal length increases, DOF decreases.

- As the sensor/film size increases, DOF decreases.

- Shot from the same location, a shorter lens on a crop sensor DSLR, gives more DOF than a DSLR with a full frame sensor.

- Shot from the same location, the same lens on a crop sensor DSLR, gives less DOF than a DSLR with a full frame sensor.

- Shot from the same location, but moving further back to get the same subject size, a crop sensor DSLR gives more DOF than a DSLR with a full frame sensor.

So why does DOF matter in photography? It provides creative control over what is in-focus or not in-focus in images. In Figure 2-5, DOF allows the subject to be isolated, blurring other elements in the image, or allows both items in the image to be in sharp focus. If a portrait has a busy background, open up the aperture to create a smaller DOF to blur the background and bring the viewer's attention to the subject. With a landscape, close down the aperture creating a larger DOF and have much more of the image in sharp focus.

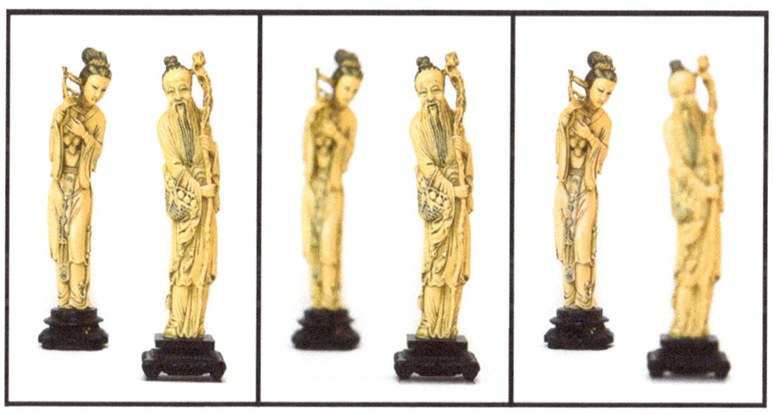

FIGURE 2-5

ACCESSORIES

Once you start to see your photographic skills advance, you'll probably want to add some accessories to enable you to produce either special effects, or more creative images in camera. One of the accessories most photographers have is a hot shoe flash. This is an external flash unit that attaches directly to the top (hot shoe) of your camera. They can range from relatively inexpensive to very expensive units and often take the place of an external studio strobe.

Then there are filters that fit over the end of the lenses you use. A few of these are:

- *Ultra-Violet (UV)* – Often used to protect the front element of a lens and it also removes the bluish color cast created by the UV light in normal daylight.

- *Polarizing* – Used to darken blue skies or remove glare from surfaces. There are two type of polarizing filters, linear and circular. Today's DSLR's only use a circular polarizing filter.

- *Graduated* – Used to darken only a portion of the scene, like a bright sky in a landscape photograph.

- *Color* – Intentionally adds a color cast to an image or makes changes for mismatched light temperature. The range of color filters runs the gamut of the rainbow.

- *Multi-Image* – Used to create special effects in camera versus post processing.

- *Neutral density* – Used to darken the entire image to allow longer exposure times for special effects. i.e. a empty highway shot at midday.

Another popular accessory is a battery grip. This supports the use of multiple batteries in the camera extending the number of shots that can be taken prior to replacing or recharging them. Secondarily, it provides additional stability of grip for those photographers with large hands.

There are too many accessories to list here, so check with your online or neighborhood camera store for more suggestions.

WORKFLOW

Workflows are the steps you consistently do in order to perform a function on/with your images. In photography there can be many workflows for a particular function.

As an example, you can have separate workflows for:

1 Copying or ingesting images to a computer.

2 Sorting, culling or editing images.

3 Printing images.

4 Sharing images via the web, albums, etc.

5 Emailing images.

6 Archiving or saving your images.

Depending on the individual, each of these workflows can be different and customized for specific needs. However, taken as a whole, all of these workflows become your general workflow for processing images.

In general, there are programs that make creating and consistently doing your workflow easier. Some of them are:

1   Picassa

2   Photoshop Elements

3   iPhoto

4   Photoshop

5   Photoshop Lightroom

6   Apple Aperture

PARTS 1 & 2 SUMMARY

Yes, there is a lot of technical information put forth in Parts 1 & 2. You don't need to memorize it or even fully understand it yet, but just being familiar with these concepts, will make you a better photographer. When you hear someone talk about light temperature, if you remember that has to do with white balance, you'll be well on the way to opening a discussing with them and open a whole new path of learning. Photographers really like to help other photographers improve their skills.

For a beginner, the most important concepts are the exposure triangle, what makes up the exposure triangle, and how to begin using those concepts to create an image. As your experience increases, your experimenting will increase and that is where the real learning takes place.

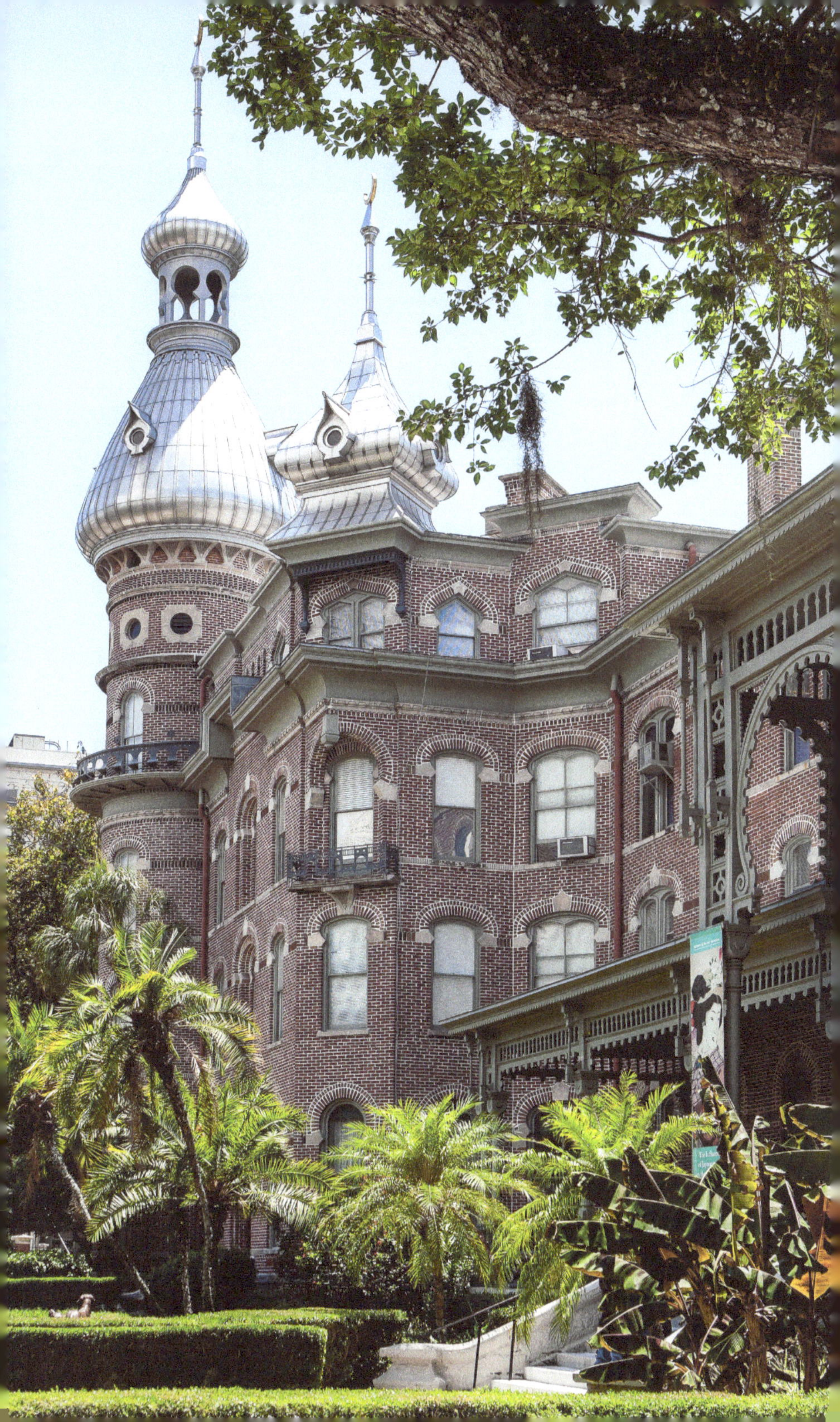

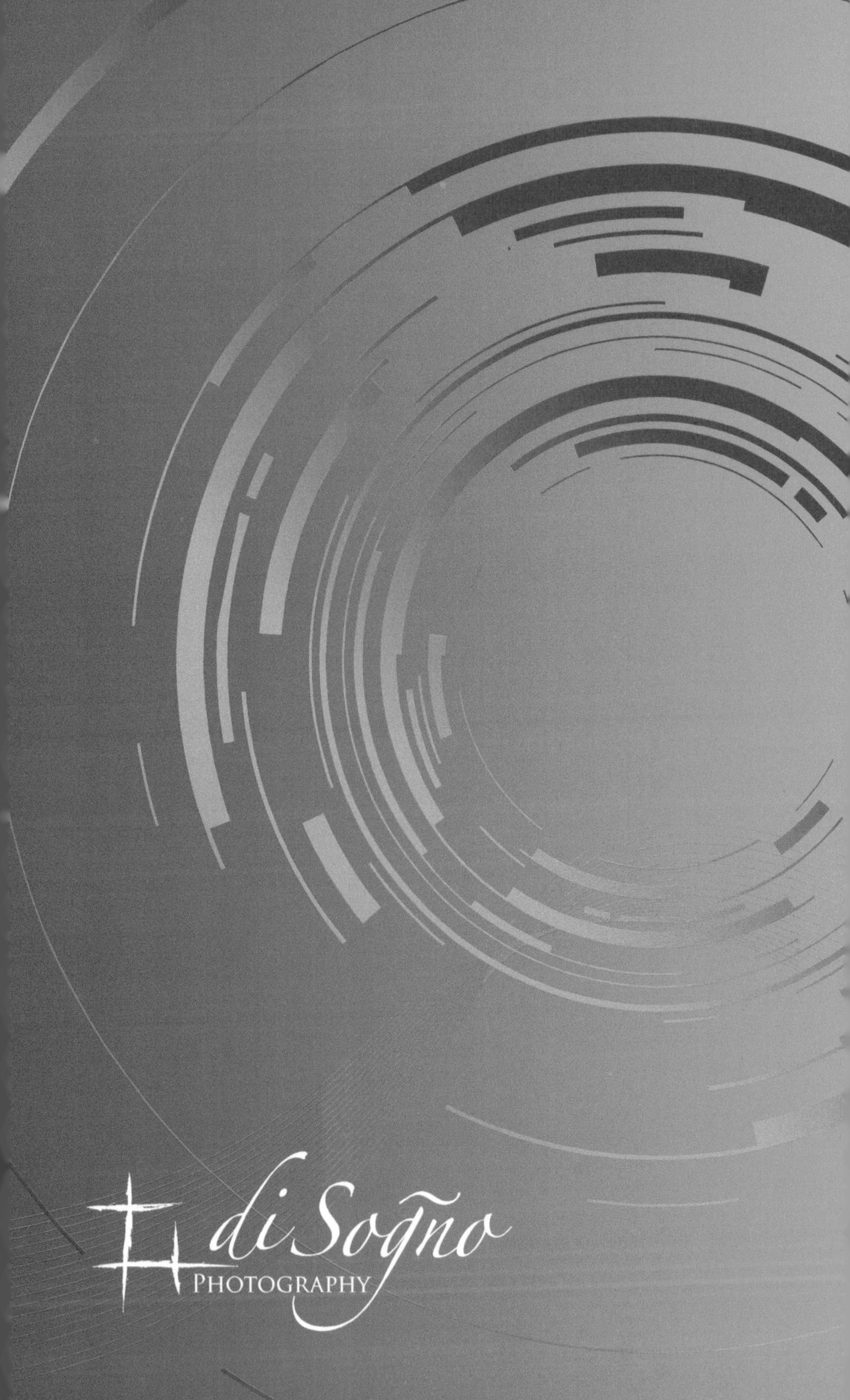
di Sogno
PHOTOGRAPHY

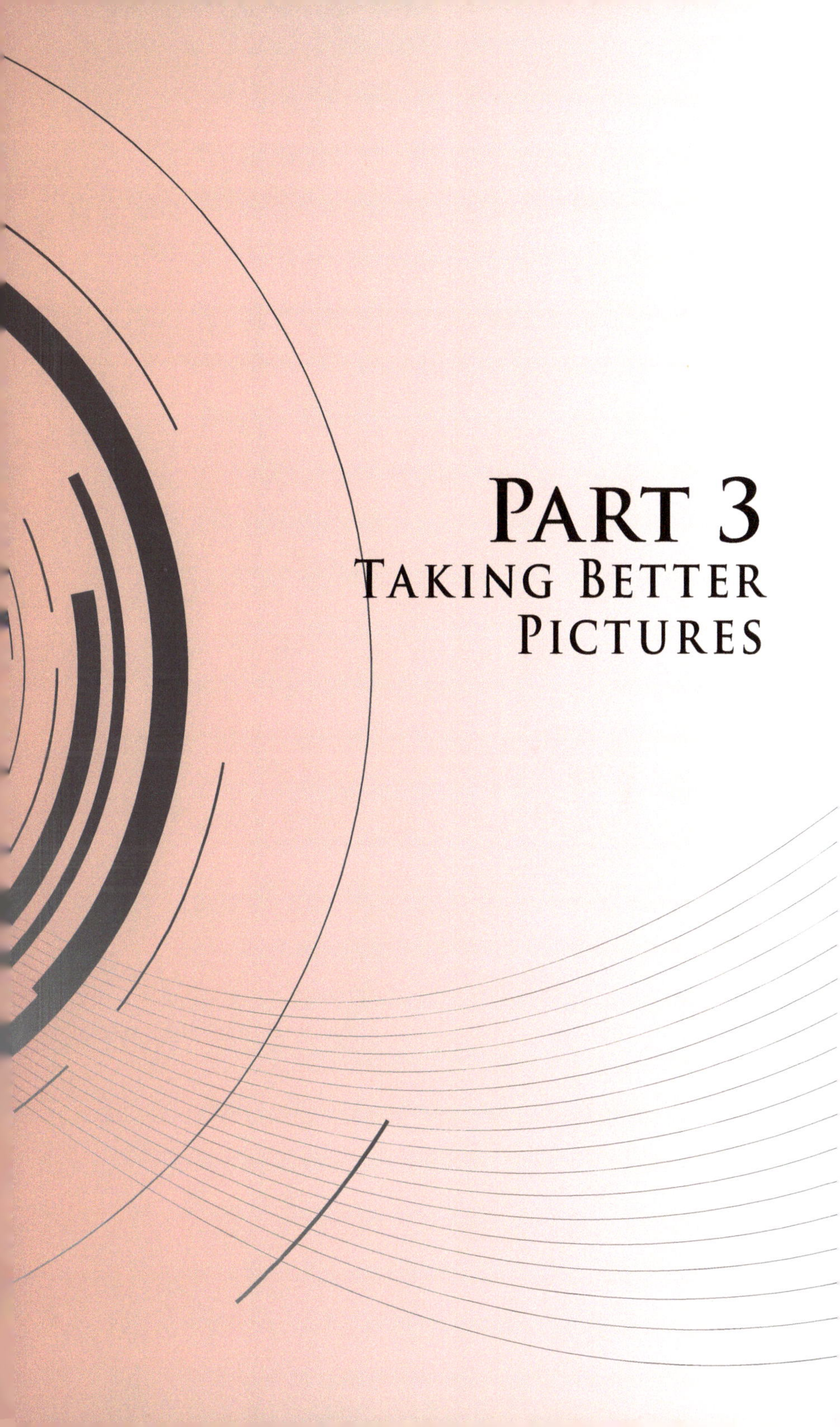

PART 3
TAKING BETTER
PICTURES

Pre-Shoot Checklist

It's always a good procedure to check your equipment prior to going out for a shoot. If you don't you may be out for a whole day and only realize at the end of the day that you didn't have a memory card in your camera or that you shot all day in the wrong white balance or worse. So it will benefit you to create a pre-shoot checklist and go over it each time you shoot.

Things to include on your checklist are:

1. *White balance* – Did you change it back to auto from that cloudy days shoot?

2. *ISO* – Did you experiment with ISO 1600 and forget to change it back to 100 prior to your daylight shoot?

3. *Exposure settings* – Do you want to be in Aperture priority or shutter priority? Manual mode or one of the auto modes?

4. *Focus mode* – One shot, AI Servo, etc.?

5. *Focus points* – Center point, auto select or manual select on another point?

6. *Batteries* – Are all batteries fully charged? Do you have any spare batteries just in case?

7. *Memory cards* – Did you bring enough memory cards with you? Have you copied the images from them to your computer prior to reformatting?

8. *Camera/Preview power off time* – is the auto off timer for the camera and the image preview on the camera's LCD set to conserve battery power?

9   *Custom settings* – Did you modify any of your custom camera settings at the last shoot and forget to reset them? i.e. Mirror lockup.

10 Do you have all of the other equipment you need for the shoot? i.e. Lens accessories, tripod, reflectors, etc.

As you can see, there is a lot to think about when you're getting ready for a shoot. So it's a good practice to create and execute a pre-shoot checklist before leaving the house.

GENERAL RULES OF IMAGE COMPOSITION

VISUALIZE THE IMAGE

One of the best ways to create a great image is to do it in your mind first. Just like a golf swing, if you visualize what you want the golf ball to do prior to addressing the ball, you'll be more likely to achieve that outcome when you swing the club and make contact. The same is true for photography. By visualizing the final image, you'll be able to take the proper tools out of the camera bag, and use them to create the image you visualized. Even if you still need to make modifications in post processing, you'll at least have most of the image created in camera, lowering the amount of time you'll need in post processing.

RULE OF THIRDS

This is the rule that is broken most often causing good images to be just snap shots. Many people who don't understand this rule will center their subject in the center of the viewfinder resulting in a mediocre image. When looking through your viewfinder, imagine two vertical lines about 1/3 and 2/3 of the way from the left of the screen as well as two horizontal lines about 1/3 and 2/3 down from the top of the screen (see Figure 3-1). Where these lines intersect is normally where the subject of the photograph should be.

FIGURE 3-1

With portraits of people, the viewers' attention is always drawn to the eyes first. It's common practice to ensure that the eyes are essentially on the line that is 1/3 from the top. Depending on the subject, it's not always possible to place it at one of the intersections. When you can't, place your subject on one of the other lines and you will still have a great image.

The Biltmore House in Asheville, NC, (Figure 3-2) is placed directly on the Rule of Thirds in the image creating a very pleasing scene.

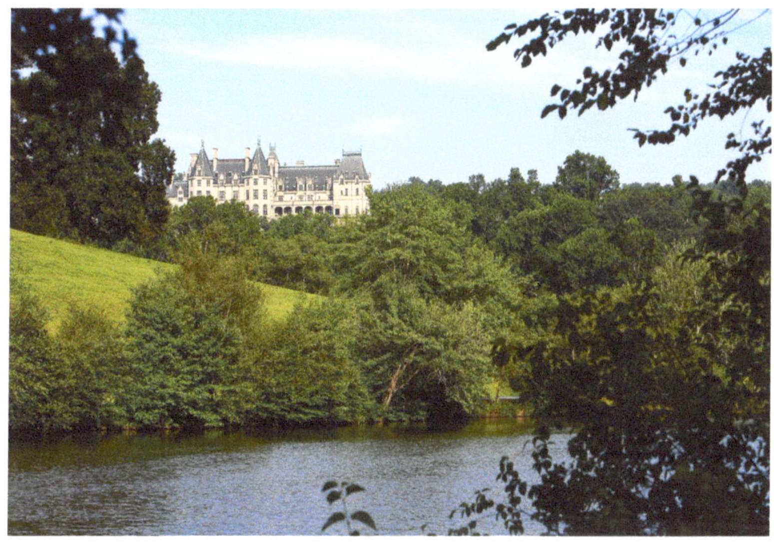

FIGURE 3-2

HAVE A SUBJECT

Often times it's difficult to determine the subject of a photo. Whenever you're shooting, have a definitive subject so that the viewer won't be wondering, "What's the subject?" or "Why did you create this image?"

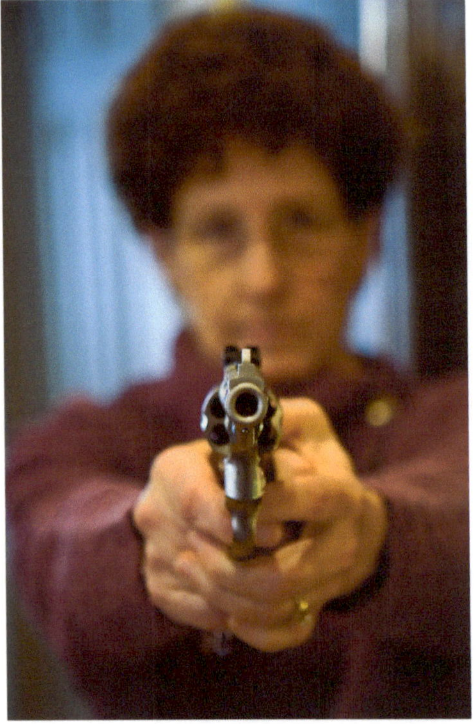

FIGURE 3-3

With the image in Figure 3-3, the subject is quite clear, and it's easy to determine that someone is going to have a bad day! It also uses another Rule of Composition called selective focus. It is accomplished by using a shallow depth of field.

FILL THE FRAME

Make sure you fill the frame with your subject. Too much space around your subject can take the viewer away from the intended focus of the image. As you can see in Figures 3-4 and 3-5, both are very nice and could look good on a desk or a wall. But the image in Figure 3-4 has too much space around the subject and will cause the viewer to look away from the subject to see what's back there. Because the image in Figure 3-5 fills the frame of the photograph, it keeps your attention where it should be and really shows off the eyes and the fantastic smile of the subject.

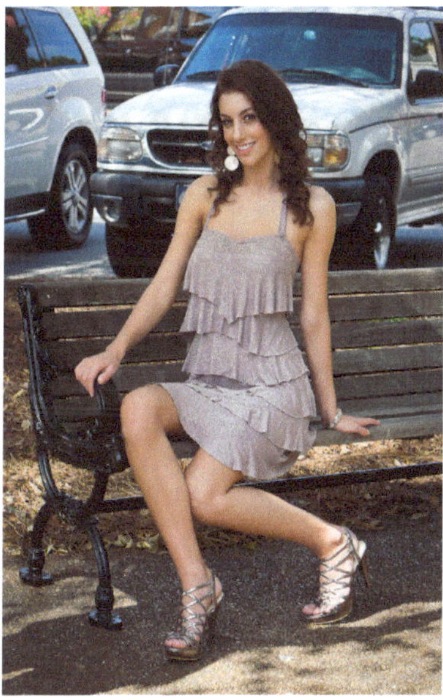

FIGURE 3-4

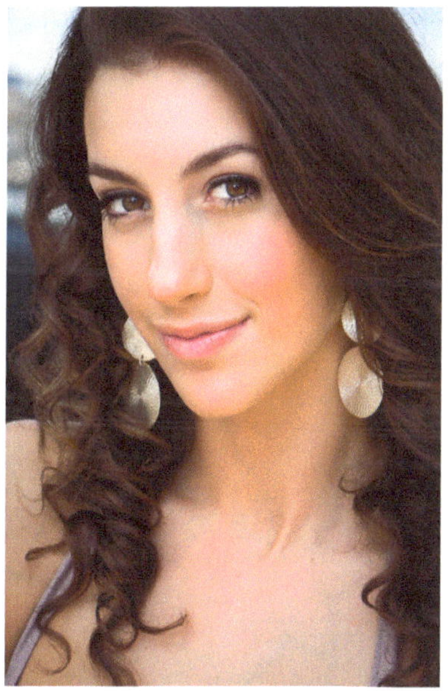

FIGURE 3-5

You'll also notice that the subject isn't directly facing the camera. She's turned a little more than 45 degrees away giving a very pleasing and thinning effect to the image.

HORIZON – WHERE TO PLACE IT

The general Rule of Composition here is to not put your horizon in the center of the image. Put it on or near either the 1/3 or 2/3 composition line. Figures 3-6 and 3-7 are two views of the same image. Figure 3-6 is a general snapshot of a beach in southern California. Note in particular that the horizon in that image is in the middle of the photo and the subjects are centered.

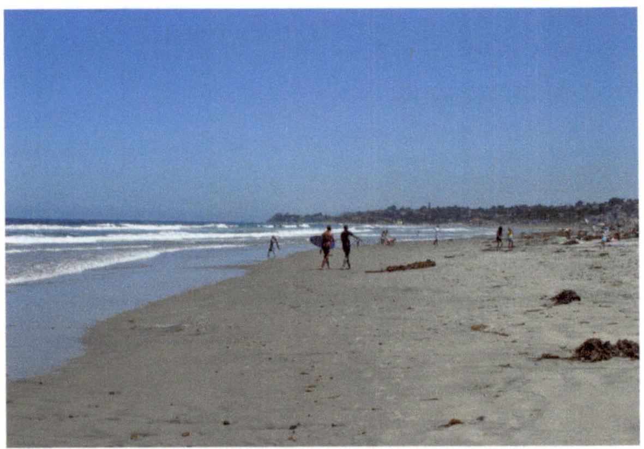

FIGURE 3-6

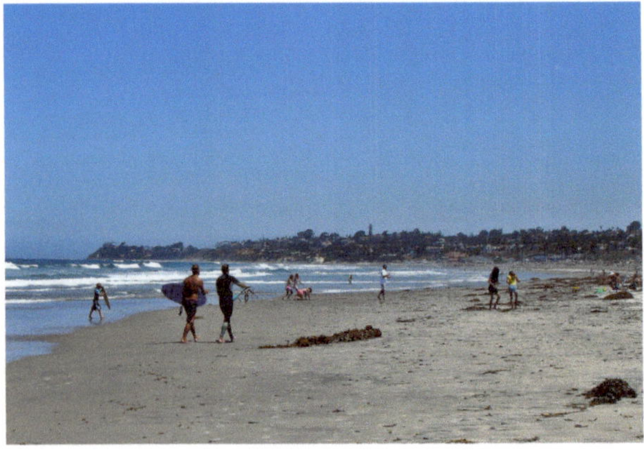

FIGURE 3-7

Figure 3-7 is a crop of the image in Figure 3-6 fixed using the Rules of Composition. The surfers are placed according to the Rule of Thirds, and doing this has brought the horizon closer to the 2/3 line. It's a much more pleasing photograph and easier for the viewer to get a sense of and be a part of what is happening on the beach. If you want to put more emphasis on the upper part of the image, the horizon should be near the 2/3 line, and by placing it at the 1/3 line, you emphasize the bottom part of the image.

FRAMING THE SUBJECT

Figure 3-8 is more interesting not only because the trees on the left and right of the image have an interesting texture, but also because the tree trunks form a frame around the model, forcing the viewer's attention onto her. Without these framing elements, the viewer's eye would wander to the trees and shrubs in the background rather than focusing on the model.

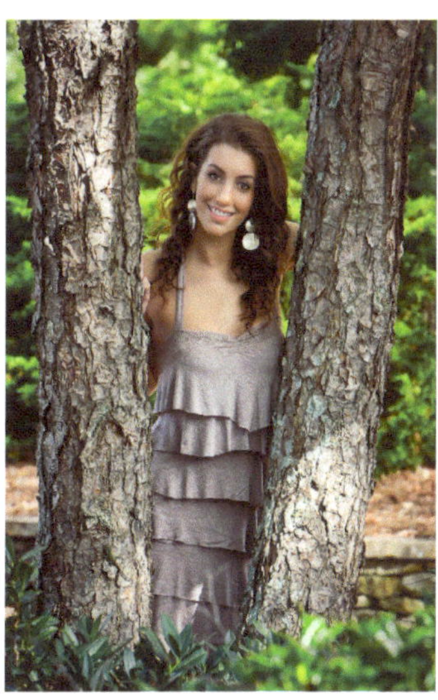

FIGURE 3-8

LEAVE SOME SPACE

This Rule of Composition generally states that you should leave space for the subject to move into or through the frame of the image. If the subject is a person running from left to right, the right side should have space for the subject to run. Otherwise it looks as though the subject is running out of the photo.

Space makes the subject look comfortable. With the image in Figure 3-9, the additional space on the right places the subject on the Rule of Thirds and gives a pleasant balance to the photo. This could become a magazine cover with text on the right side.

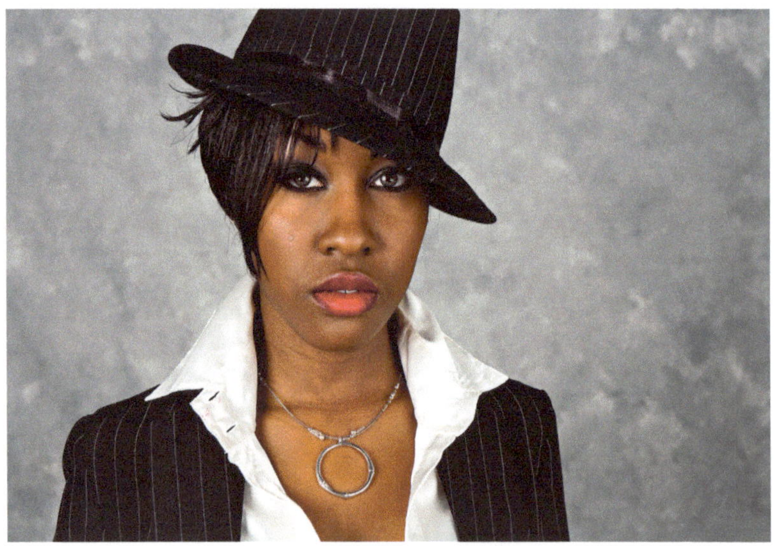

FIGURE 3-9

LEADING LINES

Leading lines are lines that draw your attention in to the photograph and lead your eyes through it. They can go horizontally, vertically, or diagonally through the image, bringing the viewers attention to where you want it to be. The image in figure 3-10 demonstrates the rule of Leading Lines. The grasses around the edge of the image lead the viewers' attention directly to the subject of the image.

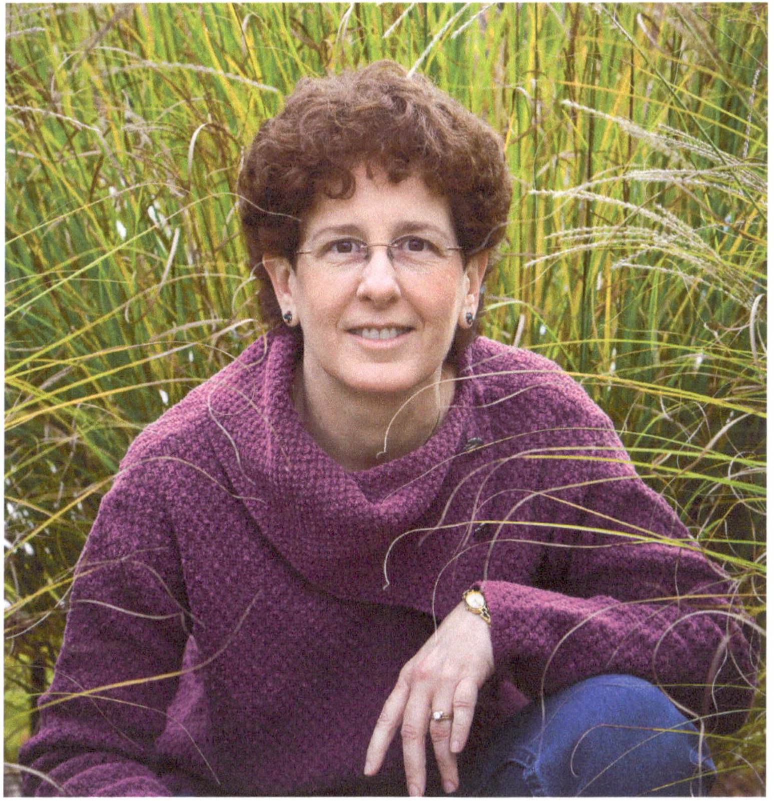

FIGURE 3-10

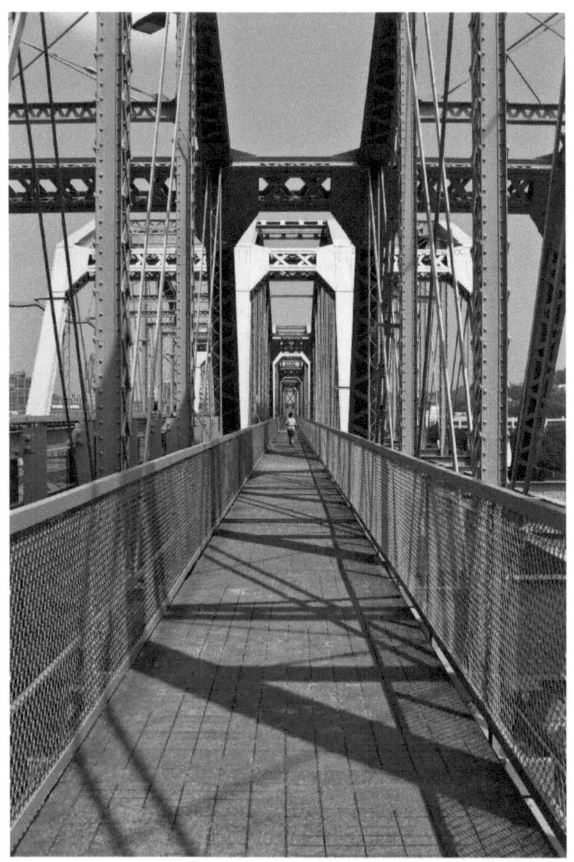

The image in Figure 3-11 is an example of converging leading lines, bringing the viewers attention to the center of image. Leading lines can be anything as long as they lead the viewer into the subject of the image.

REPETITION

Repeating items in a photograph is a good way to keep the viewers attention in the photograph and to make the image interesting. The images in Figures 3-12 and 3-13 show this by repeating the same elements multiple times creating a pleasant effect.

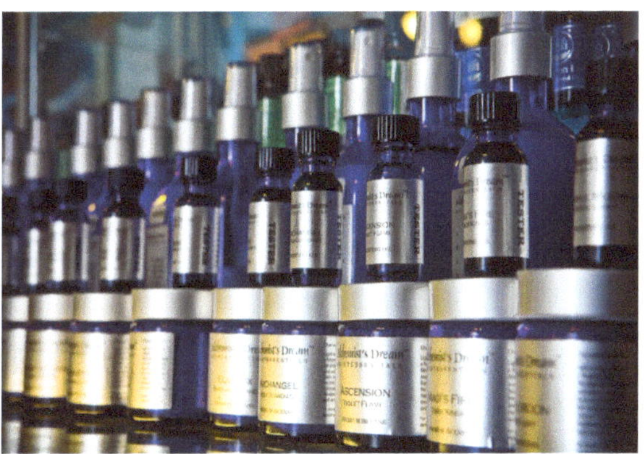

FIGURE 3-12

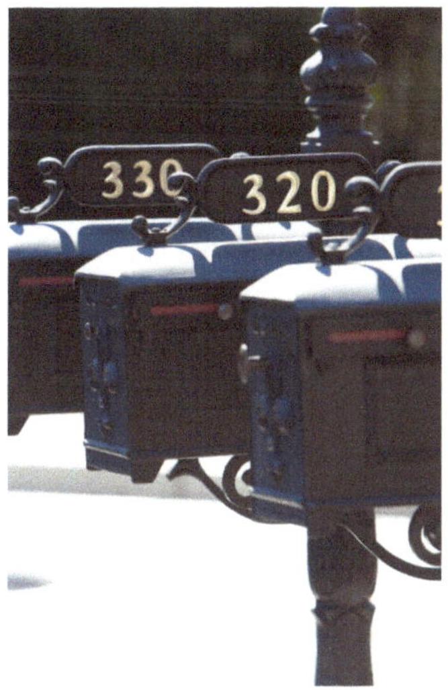

FIGURE 3-13

Panning to Show Movement

Panning is a technique that is used to show motion. When you pan the camera, you move the camera at the same speed as your subject in order to keep them in focus and blur everything else. This is a very effective way to show motion in a still image as you can see in the image of the cyclist, Figure 3-14. When panning your camera, you need to ensure that you have the focus point pre-set and that you continue to move smoothly with your subject when squeezing the shutter button. If you stop when squeezing the shutter, there is a risk that the moving subject will blur, ruining the shot.

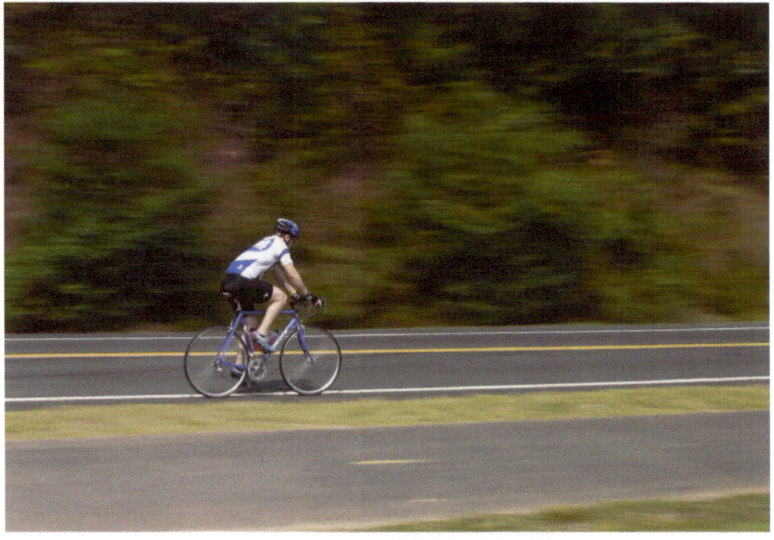

FIGURE 3-14

FILL FLASH

Have you ever looked at one of your pictures and the background had a great exposure, but the subject of the image was dark? That's because the camera was fooled by the brighter background into thinking that that's what you wanted to photograph, not that 'stuff' in the foreground. How do you fix this? You may have to override your camera settings and force it to fire the flash. Not as the primary light, but just enough to 'fill in' the dark areas of the foreground. This is called 'Fill Flash'.

In Figure 3-15, the bright background behind this subject will fool your camera and cause it to underexpose the woman's face. By activating the flash unit, enough light was provided to fill in her face and create an acceptable image.

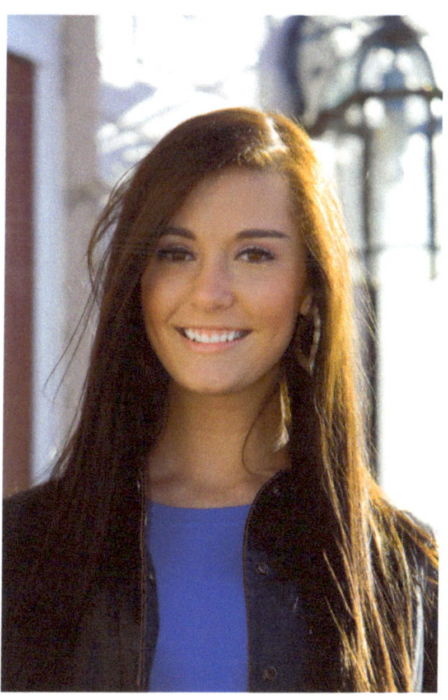

FIGURE 3-15

The image in Figure 3-16 had a strong side light causing the woman's hair to make a deep shadow on the right side of her face. By using flash to fill in the shadows, her face had the same exposure as the background.

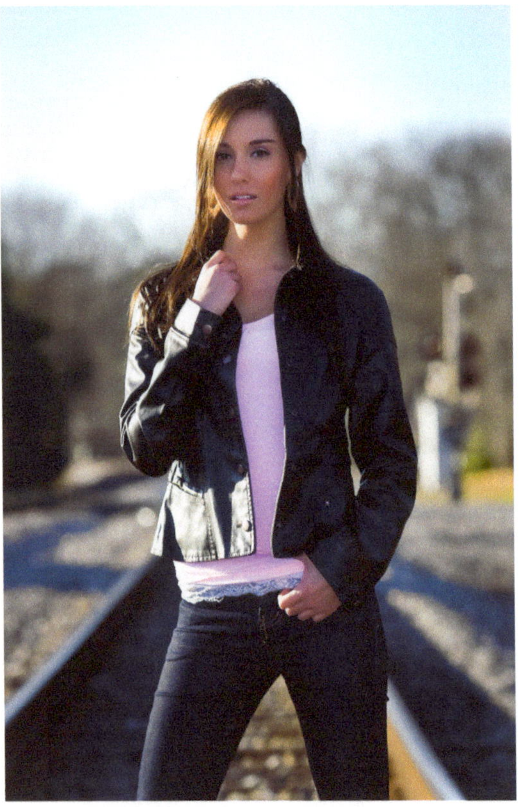

FIGURE 3-16

An added benefit of using fill flash in daylight is that it adds 'catch lights' to the eyes of your subjects. There is nothing worse than looking at a picture of someone with dark, lifeless eyes because the photographer didn't turn on their fill flash.

DISTRACTIONS IN THE IMAGE? REMOVE THEM.

The images in Figures 3-17 thru 3-19 demonstrate ways to remove distractions in an image.

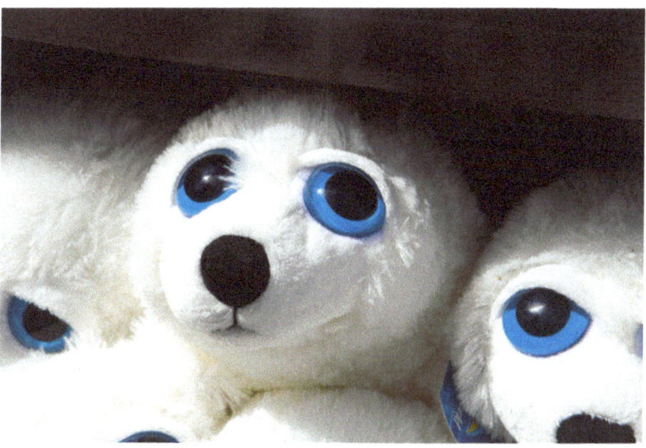

FIGURE 3-17

In Figure 3-17, the main subject is the center stuffed fur seal animal. To remove the majority of distractions, crop the image in camera using the rule of thirds to highlight the subject.

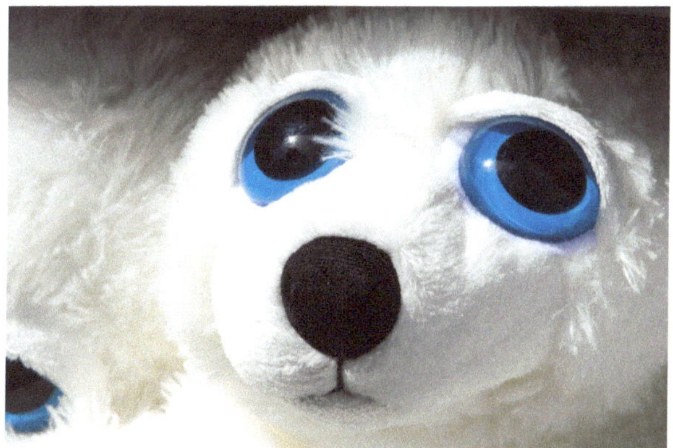

FIGURE 3-18

Cropping in camera results in a much better image (Figure 3-18) but it could be better still. The eye in the lower left of Figure 3-18 is still distracting. This is fixed in post processing by using editing software's 'clone stamp' or 'patch tool' to remove the distracting eye.

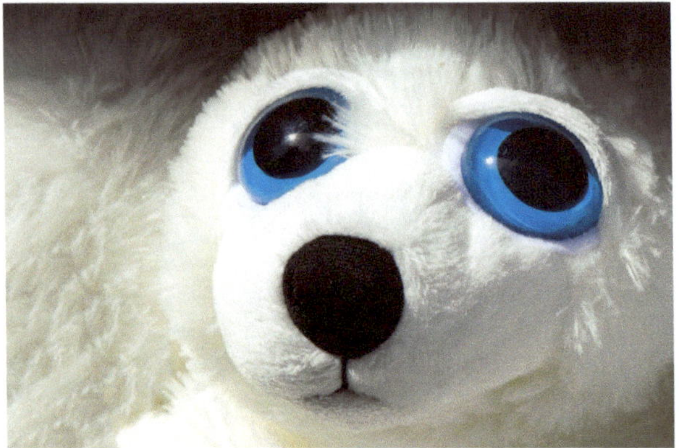

FIGURE 3-19

There are no distractions in the final image (Figure 3-19), It creates emotion in the viewer even though it's a stuffed animal.

PICTURES LOOKING LIKE A CLICHÉ? USE A DIFFERENT ANGLE, TIME OF DAY

When you create pictures try not to duplicate ones that everyone has seen before. If you do want to duplicate some famous image, don't stop there.

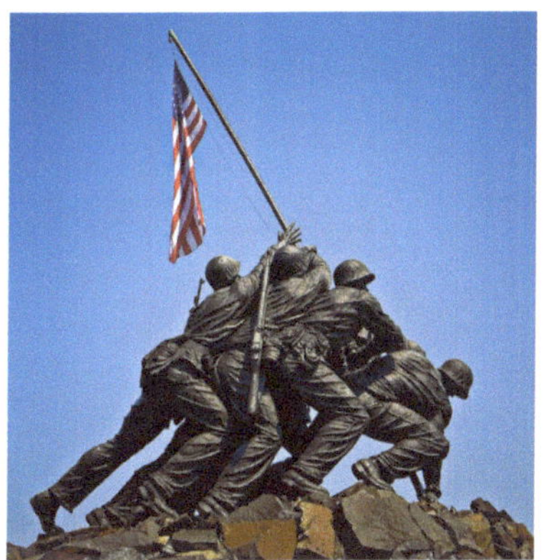

FIGURE 3-20

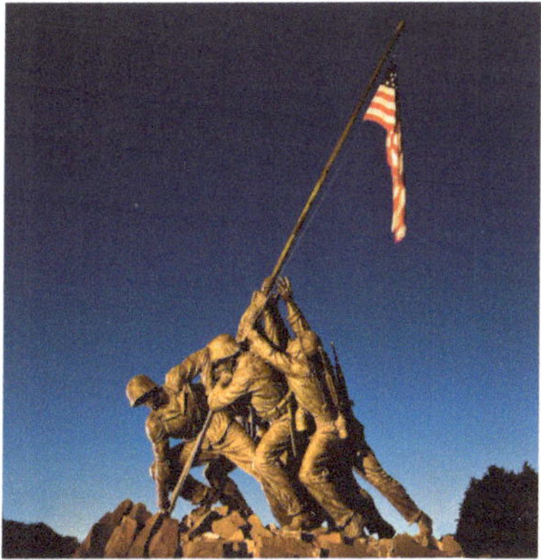

FIGURE 3-21

The Marine Corp War Memorial image in Figure 3-2- is just another picture of a statue, just like the ones you've seen for years. But by moving to a different side and returning at dusk, a fresh image of the landmark is created in Figure 3-21.

SHOOT AT NIGHT

Night photography (Figure 3-22) is a challenge but can yield some very interesting images. The trick here is that you must balance shutter speed with the movement of your subjects. A tripod is required as your exposures will be long, too long for hand-holding the camera. At night, movement can create interesting light trails and/or highly saturated colors. Trial and error though, is part of the fun of night photography.

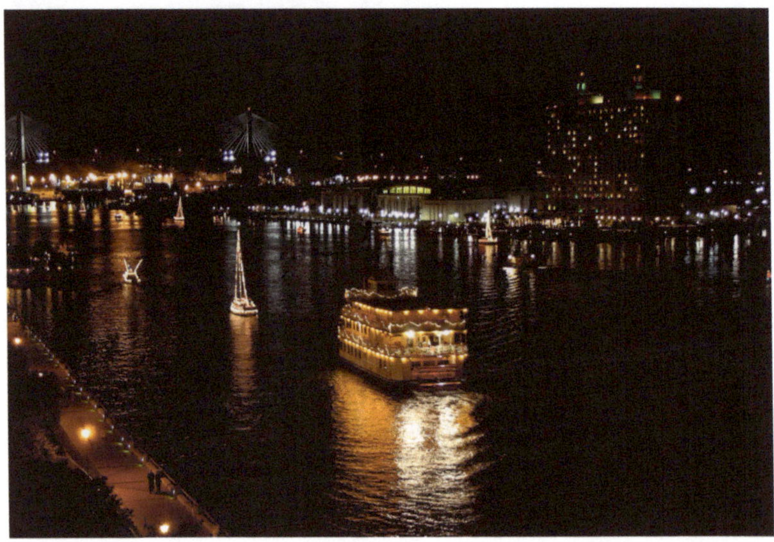

FIGURE 3-22

LOOK FOR SOMETHING INTERESTING TO SHOOT

Anything that's out of the ordinary can make a great picture and, sometimes, they make the best memories from your travels. The artwork in Figure 3-23 is found in a museum in Washington DC. It is a very unique way of using license plates from each of the fifty states and the District of Columbia to present the preamble to the constitution.

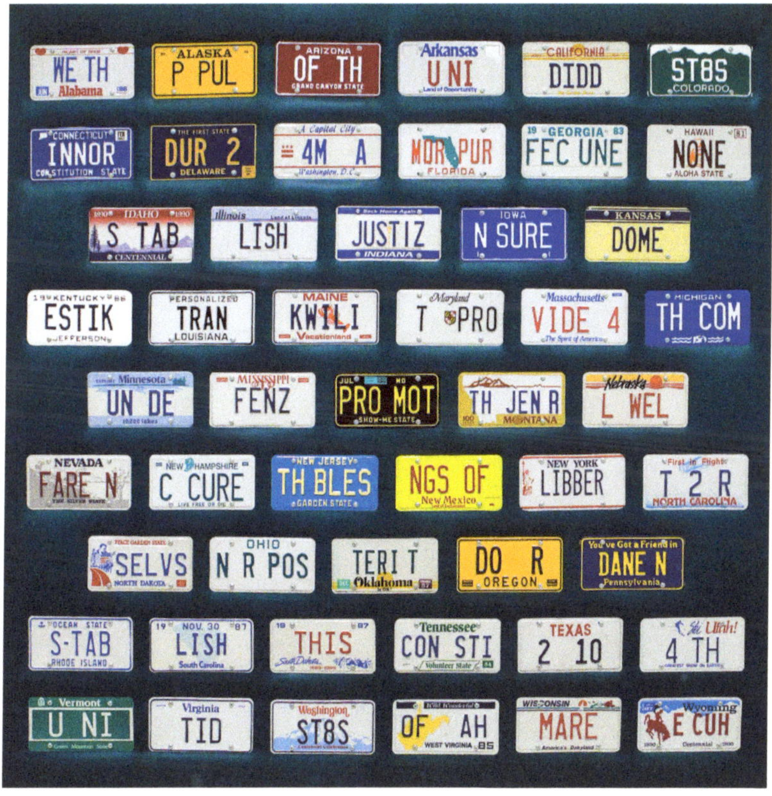

FIGURE 3-23

Tell a Story with Your Images

Your images can tell a story if you press the shutter at the right time or set up the shot. The image of the Marilyn Monroe impersonator, Figure 3-24, was intentionally posed to have her looking longingly at the jewelry store window. Everyone understands her body language and that she's telling her escort "That's so beautiful, would you buy that for me!"

The image in Figure 3-25 plainly says that the woman, whose arm is in danger, was set up. The knife wielding lab tech is having way too much fun slicing the arm of her subject while the emcee acknowledges the deed with the audience.

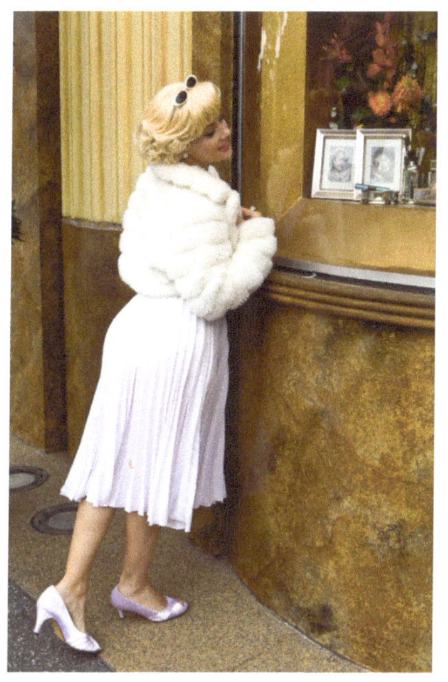

FIGURE 3-24

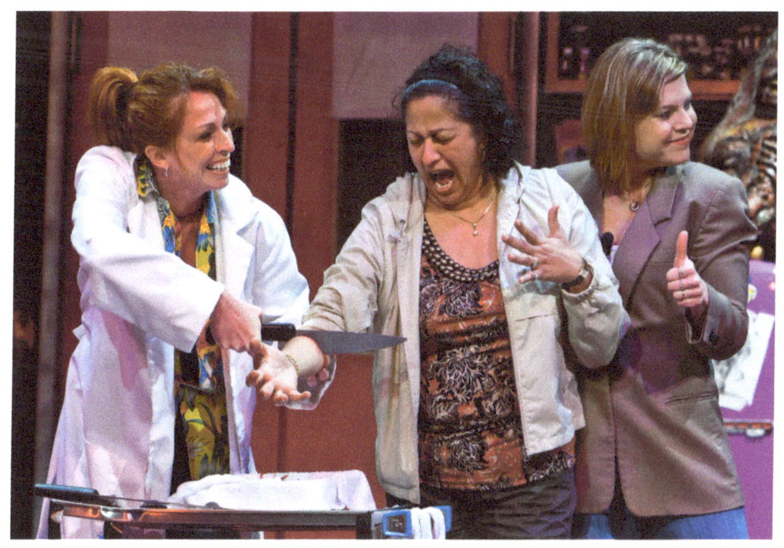

FIGURE 3-25

SELF ASSIGNMENTS – SPEED, MOTION, COLOR, ALONE

To keep your skills sharp and stay in practice, create assignments that you can shoot. A good way to do that is to just use one word assignments. Shoot out the window of a moving car to show "speed", Figure 3-26. Panning the camera with a slow shutter speed will show 'motion', Figure 3-27. The various peppers describe 'color', Figure 3-28, and a single lemon in a batch of limes embodies 'alone', Figure 3-29.

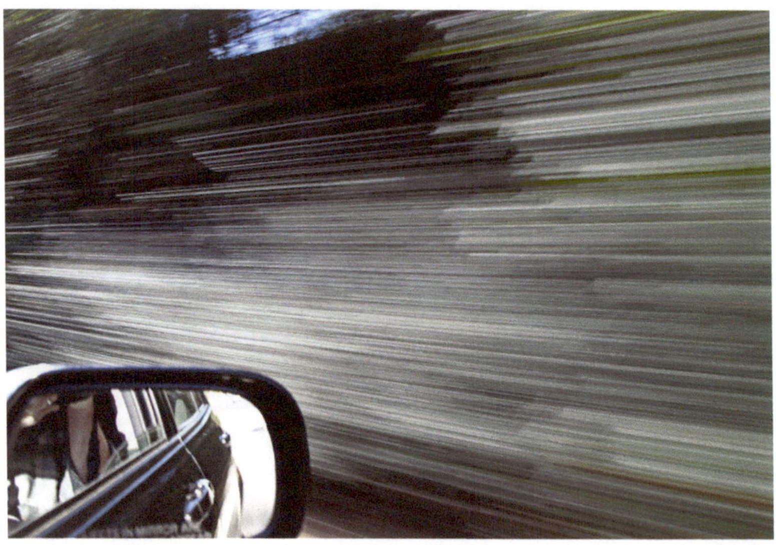

FIGURE 3.26

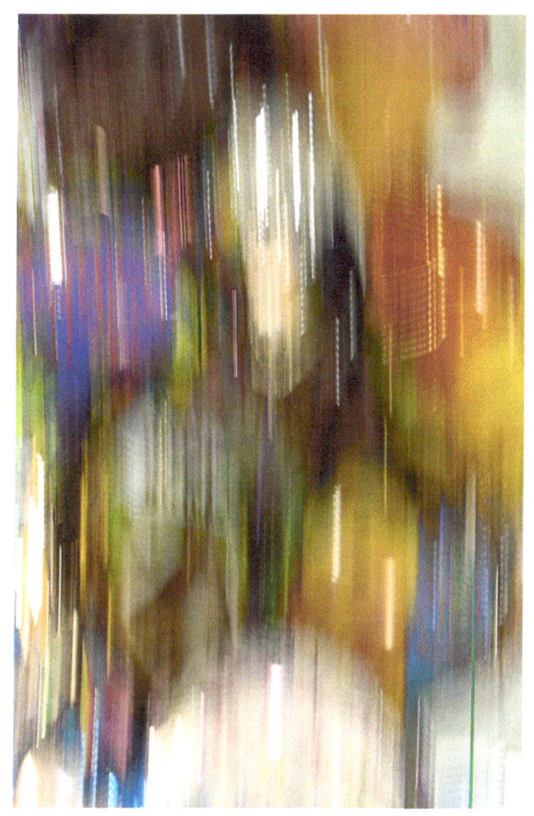

FIGURE 3-27

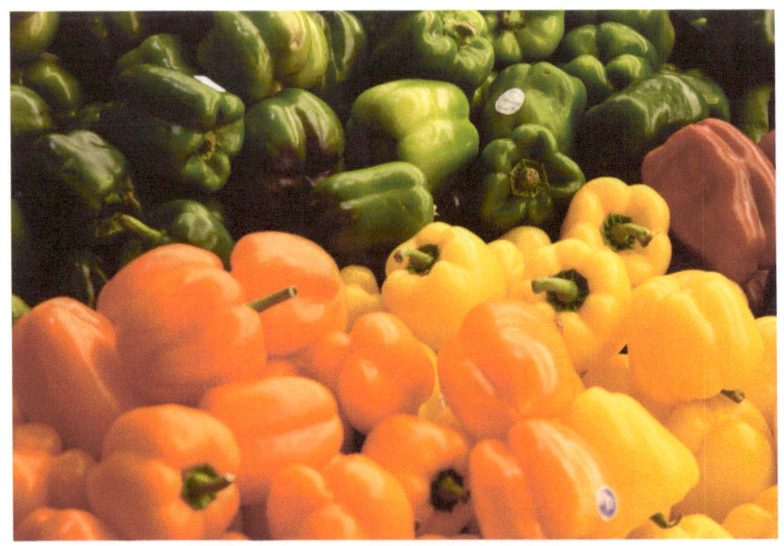

FIGURE 3-28

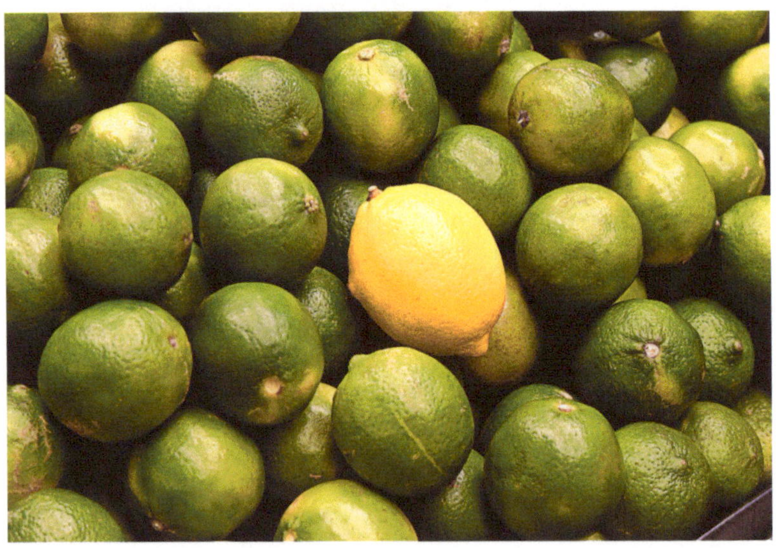

FIGURE 3-29

PART 3 SUMMARY

Part 3 presented some of the basic rules of photographic composition. There are more, but if you remember only half of these on the first few forays out to create better pictures, you will have succeeded. Once these rules become second nature to you, you can then start to consciously break them in order to create visual tension in a photo that takes it from good to great.

By visualizing your pictures and remembering to utilize these techniques, your photography will attain new heights!

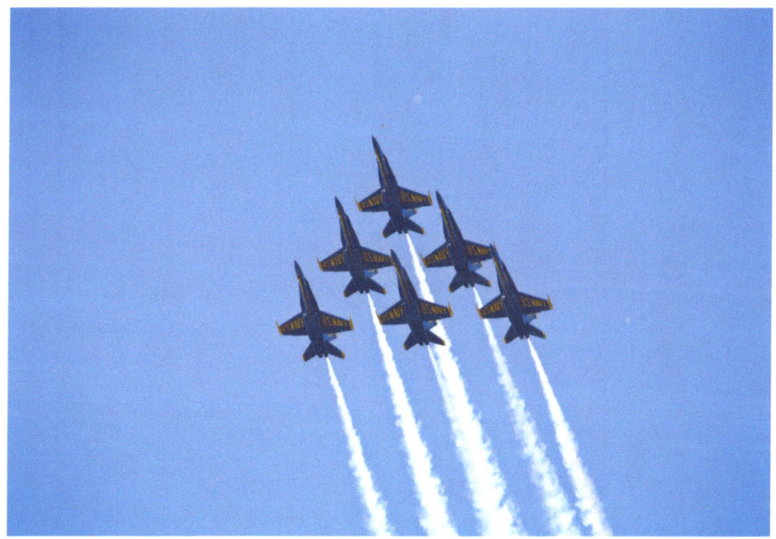

FIGURE 3-30

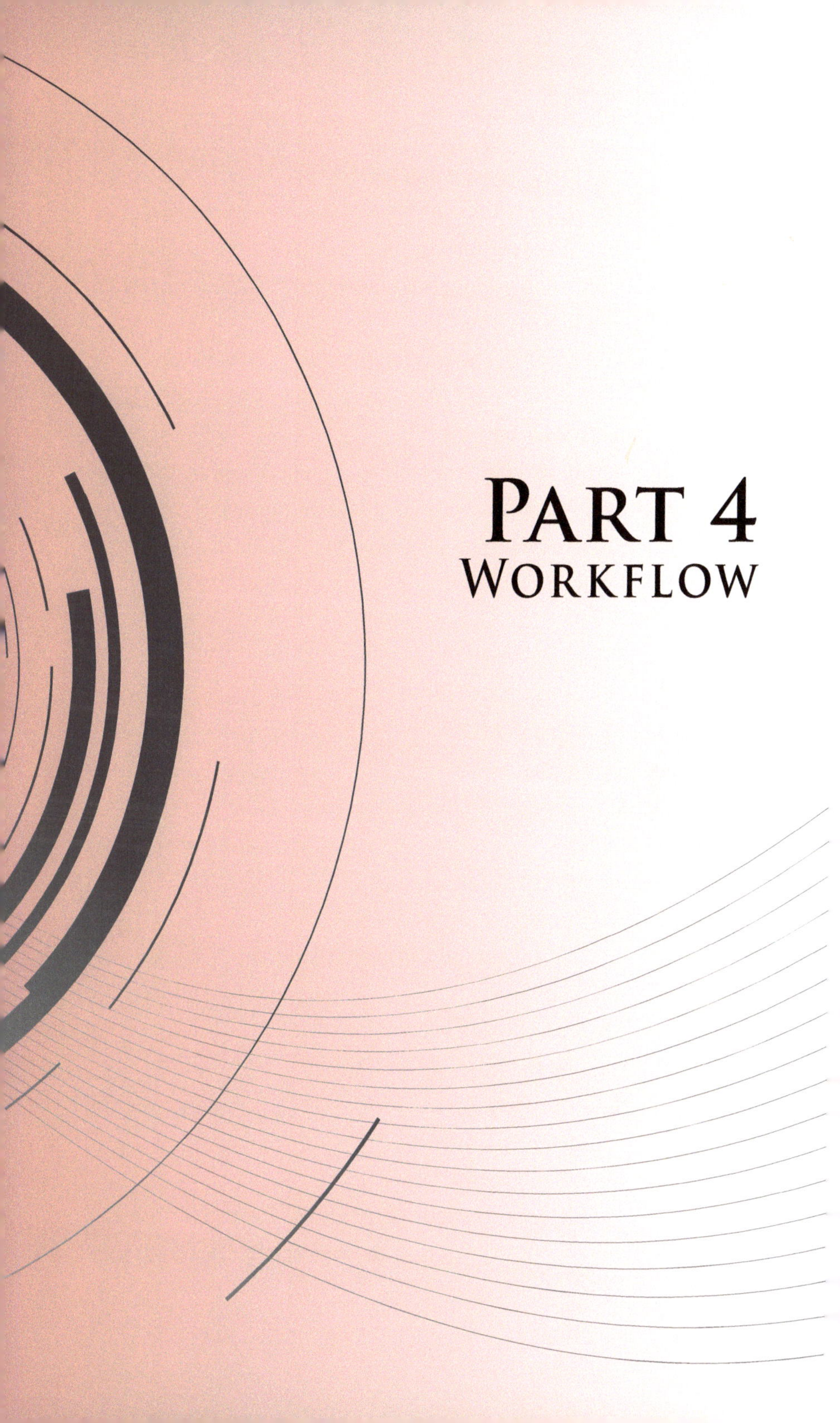

PART 4
WORKFLOW

Now that you've created the image, what do you do with it? What's next? It needs to move from the memory card to the computer so it can be edited with imaging software and create the final image that was envisioned when this process started. In order to do this, a workflow is needed.

Workflow is defined as a set of steps that are followed each time to create a final image. In other words, steps in a production line to produce the final image.

Here is a workflow that many photographers use in order to store, retrieve and process the images they've captured. Yours will probably be different because as with all things in life, if there is one way to do something, there are 100 ways of doing that thing to end up with the same result.

SAMPLE WORKFLOW OUTLINE AND DISCUSSION

1) A general post processing workflow
   a) Import images from memory card
      i) Leave card in camera or use an external reader?
         (1) Benefits/drawbacks
      ii) Rename on import
         (1) _MG.43561.CR2 becomes 110214-HEdwards-001.CR2
         (2) Why? So you can find it easier.
      iii) File organization
         (1) A personal choice to ensure you can find the image you want
            (a) All in one folder (Pictures)
            (b) Main folder, year, month, day, shoot, number
            (c) Main folder, shoot, month, day, year, number

        iv) Make backups/duplicates of images

            (1) Why?

            (2) Where to place the backups/duplicates.

            (3) May be done on import – depends on program.

b) Format the memory card in camera

    i) Start editing process

        (1) Make choices – Define the ones you like.

            (a) Flag as picks or rate them with color or stars

    ii) Delete definite clunkers

    iii) Edit the individual files for your end use.

c) Output/share/email images

    i) Print to photo printer

    ii) Upload to web based album

    iii) Upload to create a printed album

    iv) Prep image for attachment or imbed in an email

d) Archive/remove images from your hard drive

    i) How long to keep images on a hard drive.

    ii) What to backup to?

        (1) External hard drive

        (2) Removable DVD or CD

        (3) Online backup service.

PROGRAMS USED IN SAMPLE WORKFLOW

This section highlights individual programs that can be used in a professional photographic workflow to maintain a steady and repeatable production line for the final images.

PROGRAMS

1. Import – PhotoMechanic -
   http://www.camerbits.com
   a. Supports variables for metadata manipulation
      i. Information relating to the contents of a file
      ii. Stored in the file itself or in XMP sidecar file
   b. IPTC info (International Press Telecommunications Council)
   c. Key wording
   d. Make backups during import
   e. Fast browser that supports:
      i. Flags
      ii. Stars
      iii. Color codes

2. File organization/global edits – Lightroom –
   http://www.adobe.com
   a. DAM – Digital Asset Manager
   b. Editing to best images
      i. Flags
      ii. Stars
      iii. Color codes

    c.   Make global changes to file
- i.   Non-destructive
- ii.   Graduated filters, spot removal, adjustment brush
- iii.   Cropping

    d.   Output to multiple file types
- i.   Benefits of each file type
    1. PSD (Photoshop Document)
        a. Large
        b. Lossless
        c. Supports layers
    2. JPEG (Joint Photographic Experts Group)
        a. Small to large
        b. Lossy compression
        c. Doesn't support layers
        d. Universal standard
    3. TIFF (Tagged Image File Format)
        a. Large
        b. Supports layers
        c. Universal standard
        d. Supports Lossless compression

    e.   Print creation

3. Bit fiddling or pixel editing program
    a. Photoshop – *http://www.adobe.com*
        i. Creates large files
        ii. Pixel editing, cloning, masking, layers, etc.
        iii. Destructive unless non-destructive workflow technique is used
        iv. Removing objects, changing heads, etc.

4. Plug-ins – add-ons to Lightroom or Photoshop that do specific functions

   a. Ron Nichols Studio Palettes – scripts to set up PS -
       http://www.ronnichols.com

   b. onOne Software -
       http://www.ononesoftware.com

       i. Perfect Photo Suite

           1. PhotoFrames – Edge and framing effects

           2. Genuine Fractals – now Perfect Resize 7 – Resize images for print

           3. Focal Point – Selective focus

           4. Mask Pro 4 – Removing backgrounds

   c. Nik Software -
       http://www.google.com/nikcollection

       i. Color EFex Pro Complete - > Special effects filters

       ii. Viveza 2 – Light and Color adjustments

       iii. Silver EFex Pro 2 – B&W Conversions

   d. Imagenomic -
       http://www.imagenomic.com

       i. Portaiture – Skin softening

Summary

The workflows presented here are the ones the author uses. Workflows are very customizable items in the process of creating pictures. All of the various software add-ons, applications, personal preferences and their respective workflows are used to create the final image but, what works for one photographer may not work for another. Make them your own.

BIOGRAPHY

After receiving his Electrical Engineering degree in the late 1970's, Tony worked in the computer field specializing in systems repair and network design for a handful of Fortune 500 companies. During his business travels he carried his camera with him to document not only what he had done, but to capture the beauty of the areas he visited. He began a life-long study of the technical aspects of photography to showcase the wonderful locations he was seeing.

In 2003 camera manufacturers put a lens on a computer and called it a digital camera and he was hooked, so he moved to photography full time after almost 30 years in IT. Today his workflow is totally digital as he focuses on small to medium scale commercial photography clients providing executive portraiture, product images and architectural views of the business locations.

Tony is an active membership of the Professional Photographers of America (PPA) to keep his skills up-to-date and learn new photographic techniques. He attends continuing education classes and seminars presented by modern day legends of photography and regularly networks with other professional photographers. In 2011 he started teaching the basics of photography to first time DSLR owners to pass on his knowledge and love of photography to amateur photographers.

INDEX

A

aperture 2, 6, 7, 10, 16, 19, 21,
        24, 25, 27, 36, 38, 39, 40,
        41
ASA 16, 17

B

Basic Zone 10
Bokeh 38
Breathing 15

C

CCD 8
Changing the Lens 11
Close-up 10
CMOS 8
Creative Zone 10
Cropping 64, 79
crop sensor 8, 40, 41

D

depth of field 2, 24, 38, 52
DIN 16, 17
DOF 39, 40, 41

E

Exposure 16, 27, 48
Exposure Value 27

F

fill flash 62
focal length 8, 19, 36, 37, 38, 39,
        40
f-stop 19, 40

full frame sensor 8, 40, 41

H

horizon 54, 55

I

incident light meter 31
ISO 2, 16, 17, 25, 27, 48

J

JPEG 2, 33, 79

L

landscape 41, 42
law of reciprocity 16
LCD 12, 48
Leading Lines 57
lenses 2, 36, 37, 38, 42
lens speed 21, 38
light meter 30, 31, 32

M

manual 6, 10, 14, 25, 48
Mirror 6, 49
motion 12, 23, 60, 70

N

Night photography 66

P

Panning 60, 70
Pentaprism 6
Photographic Stop 25
portrait 41

Pre-Shoot Checklist 48
Programs 33, 78

R

Raw 33
reflected light meter 31
Repetition 59
Rule of Thirds 50, 51, 55, 56

S

selective focus 52
Sensor 6, 8
shutter 2, 6, 7, 10, 12, 14, 15, 16,
        17, 19, 21, 22, 23, 25, 27,
        38, 48, 60, 66, 68, 70
shutter speed 2, 10, 16, 19, 21,
        22, 23, 25, 27, 66, 70
shutter speeds 17, 21, 22
subject 24, 32, 36, 38, 40, 41, 50,
        52, 53, 56, 57, 58, 60, 61,
        63, 68

T

telephoto lens 36, 38
tripod 12, 23, 49, 66

V

viewfinder 6, 12, 14, 19, 32, 50

W

white balance 2, 27, 28, 44, 48
wide angle lens 36
Workflow 43, 75, 76

Z

zoom lens 36